# Weekly Lesson Tests Copying Masters

## Teacher Edition
## Grade 3

### Harcourt School Publishers
www.harcourtschool.com

Printed in the United States of America

ISBN 10  0-15-351721-2     ISBN 13  978-0-15-351721-1

7 8 9 10   1413   16 15 14 13 12 11 10

# Contents

# Contents

# Contents

# Overview

Use the *Weekly Lesson Tests* to monitor students' comprehension of the Student Edition selections and progress with the skills in each lesson. Each skill area has its own test section. The sections can be given all at once, or you can administer them at different times.

## About the Test Sections

### Selection Comprehension

This section assesses the first selections in each Student Edition lesson. It includes eight multiple-choice items and one open-ended item. Each multiple-choice item is worth one point and the open-ended item is worth two points. Use the rubric below to score the open-ended item.

| 2 points | • Shows good attention to the task<br>• Clearly based on the text the student read<br>• Includes adequate support or examples<br>• Accurate and complete |
|---|---|
| 1 point | • Shows some attention to the task<br>• Somewhat based on the text the student read<br>• Includes some support or examples<br>• Contains some inaccurate or incomplete details |
| 0 points | • Shows no attention to the task<br>• Not clearly based on the text the student read<br>• Lacks support or examples<br>• Inaccurate and incomplete |

Once per theme, the open-ended item assesses comprehension of the paired selection.

### Phonics/Spelling

This section assesses students' progress with the phonics/spelling skill or skills in the lesson.

### Focus Skill

This section assesses the focus skill in the lesson.

### Additional Skills

This section assesses the additional skills in the lesson. These include vocabulary strategies, research study skills, and literary analysis skills.

## Robust Vocabulary

This section assesses the Robust Vocabulary in the lesson. Because these questions require students to think deeply about word meanings, both the teacher and students can learn a great deal by discussing students' responses and their reasoning. This not only informs the teacher of students' word knowledge, but also extends instruction and keeps students actively involved with the Robust Vocabulary. It is important to continue to engage students with these words in successive weeks, as true depth of knowledge only results from multiple, meaningful encounters with words. One way to extend this section is to have students write these words in their journals and add stars to show how well they know each word:

☆ I don't know the word.

☆☆ I know the word a little.

☆☆☆ I know the word very well.

## Grammar

This section assesses students' progress with the grammar skill in the lesson.

## Oral Reading Fluency

Assessing oral reading fluency will help you determine how well a student can apply decoding skills and recognize words quickly. Both narrative and expository passages are provided. The readability has been controlled so that the text is on grade level for students.

To administer the fluency assessment, use the Oral Reading Fluency Recording Forms on pages 9–32. Student copies of the passages are provided with each Weekly Lesson Test. All of the passages are "fresh reads" that students have not read before.

## Directions for Administering

1. Explain the task to the student. Tell the student that you want to see how well he or she can read aloud. Inform the student that you will follow along as he or she reads, taking notes. The student may ask about being timed. Encourage him or her to read at his or her "normal" pace. You don't want the student to speed up and read artificially fast because of the timing.
2. Have the student begin. Use a stopwatch or a second hand to time a one-minute interval as inconspicuously as possible.
3. As the student reads, record reading errors unobtrusively on the Recording Form. Mark mispronunciations, substitutions, omissions of a sound or word, and other errors. *Do not count repetitions or self-corrections as reading errors.*
4. When the stopwatch or second hand reaches the one-minute mark, place a slash mark on the Oral Reading Fluency Recording Form after the last word the student reads. Tell the student to stop reading.

## Computing the Fluency Score

1. Total the number of words read by the student in one minute. The row numbers in the right margin will help you determine the number quickly.
2. Count the number of reading errors the student made. Remember, do not count repetitions or self-corrections as reading errors.
3. Subtract the number of reading errors made from the total number of words read correctly. This is the student's oral reading fluency score. Write the words correctly read per minute (WCPM) on the Recording Form.

## Interpreting the Fluency Score

The norms below are based on a study conducted by Hasbrouck and Tindal (2006) in which they established fluency norms for Grades 1 through 8. Look at the WCPM norms below, finding the column that corresponds most closely to the time of year the test was given, and compare the student's score to the norms. Students reading below the 50th percentile may require additional instruction to improve oral reading fluency.

| Grade 3 Oral Reading Fluency Norms | | | |
|---|---|---|---|
| Percentile | Fall | Winter | Spring |
| 25th | 44 | 62 | 78 |
| 50th | 71 | 92 | 107 |
| 75th | 99 | 120 | 137 |

Source: Hasbrouck, Jan, and Gerald A. Tindal. 2006. Oral reading fluency norms: A valuable assessment tool for reading teachers. *Reading Teacher* 59 (April), no. 7: 636–644.

# Oral Reading Fluency

| | |
|---|---:|
| Once upon a time there was a greedy dog. Even | 10 |
| though he had plenty of food and toys, he always desired | 21 |
| more. One afternoon he observed a little puppy chewing | 30 |
| on a huge bone. | 34 |
| "Give me that bone," the greedy dog growled. The | 43 |
| frightened puppy dropped the bone and scurried away. | 51 |
| The greedy dog scooped up the bone and marched on | 61 |
| his way. | 63 |
| As the greedy dog crossed a bridge over a creek, he | 74 |
| glanced over the edge of the bridge and noticed another | 84 |
| dog staring up at him from the water. That dog also had | 96 |
| a huge bone in his mouth. The greedy dog decided he | 107 |
| wanted that bone, too. | 111 |
| He bared his teeth and let out a fierce growl. Much | 122 |
| to his disbelief, the dog in the water growled back. The | 133 |
| greedy dog snapped at the bone in the other dog's | 143 |
| mouth. Plop! The bone in the greedy dog's mouth fell | 153 |
| into the water, and the other dog vanished. | 161 |
| "That dog has stolen my bone! " thought the greedy | 170 |
| dog, "I must find him!" | 175 |
| Of course, he never did. | 180 |

# Oral Reading Fluency

| | |
|---|---:|
| Dylan was eager to begin his first camping trip. His | 10 |
| parents had packed the tent and sleeping bags in the car. | 21 |
| Dylan had borrowed a book about camping from | 29 |
| the library. He began to read the book during the trip in | 41 |
| the car. Dylan was very interested in the chapter titled | 51 |
| "Camping Safely." He carefully read the page about | 59 |
| poison ivy. | 61 |
| "The leaves grow in groups of three," Dylan read | 70 |
| aloud. "Study the picture of this poisonous plant on the | 80 |
| next page." But, someone had torn out the page with | 90 |
| the picture of the plant! | 95 |
| That afternoon, the family went for a walk in the | 105 |
| woods. Dylan counted the leaves on each plant they | 114 |
| passed. Suddenly, his brother pointed at an owl sitting | 123 |
| in a tree. Dylan forgot the plants as he stepped closer to | 135 |
| the tree. | 137 |
| "Dylan," said his mother, "You're standing in poison | 145 |
| ivy! Get out of there!" | 150 |
| Dylan looked down and counted the leaves, "One, | 158 |
| two, and three." Realizing his mistake, he turned and | 167 |
| ran back to the trail. | 172 |
| "Well, now you know what poison ivy looks like!" said | 182 |
| his dad. | 184 |

# Oral Reading Fluency

|  |  |
|---|---|
| Alex froze when he saw the clown walk into the yard. | 11 |
| He couldn't let his friends at the party know that he was | 23 |
| terrified of clowns! | 26 |
| Alex joined the group of kids who had gathered | 35 |
| around the clown. "It's just a clown," he whispered | 44 |
| to himself. | 46 |
| From behind, Alex heard someone say, "It's just a | 55 |
| clown." Worried that someone was making fun of him, | 64 |
| Alex slowly turned around. He saw a five-year-old boy, | 73 |
| sobbing quietly while his mother tried to comfort him. | 82 |
| "I think I can help," Alex said to the boy's mother. | 93 |
| She smiled gratefully and stepped aside. He bent and | 102 |
| whispered in the boy's ear, "When I was a kid," he said, | 114 |
| "I was afraid of clowns, too." | 120 |
| "You're not afraid of them now? They're so scary!" | 129 |
| the boy said. | 132 |
| "I faced my fear," Alex said. "Look at that clown. He's | 143 |
| really pretty silly if you watch him." | 150 |
| Alex and the boy watched the clown for a little while, | 161 |
| and then the boy chuckled. Alex was happy to know that | 172 |
| by helping someone else, he had learned to control his | 182 |
| own fear. | 184 |

# Oral Reading Fluency

| | |
|---|---|
| Amanda was spending the night at her friend's house. | 9 |
| Amanda and Kayla had been friends since first grade. It | 19 |
| was quiet and dark in the living room, where the girls were | 31 |
| settled in their sleeping bags. | 36 |
| Suddenly, Amanda heard a noise. Her eyes jerked open. | 45 |
| "Kayla?" she called, but Kayla was asleep. | 52 |
| Amanda listened carefully, but the noise was gone. Just | 61 |
| as her eyes grew heavy, she heard the sound again. "What | 72 |
| is that?" she asked herself. "Is it a garbage truck? No, the | 84 |
| garbage truck wouldn't come at night. Is it an airplane? No, | 95 |
| that noise was louder than an airplane." | 102 |
| Amanda thought of waking Kayla, but the noise wasn't | 111 |
| scary. It was just loud. She clicked on the flashlight she and | 123 |
| Kayla had used earlier for reading. Slowly, she crawled out | 133 |
| of her sleeping bag. | 137 |
| As she walked toward the kitchen, the noise grew louder. | 147 |
| Amanda shone the beam around the kitchen. The noise was | 157 |
| very loud in here! Suddenly, she froze in her tracks! Then she | 169 |
| started laughing. Kayla's dog, Ruffy, was snoring! Amanda | 177 |
| laughed again and went back to the living room. | 186 |

# Oral Reading Fluency

|  |  |
|---|---|
| Have nurses ever held your wrist and told you to be | 11 |
| quiet? If so, do you know what they were doing and why | 23 |
| it was important? | 26 |
| You probably know that your heart pumps blood. Did | 35 |
| you know that blood travels in tubes, called arteries, from | 45 |
| your heart to all parts of your body? Some of these tiny | 57 |
| tubes are in your wrist. | 62 |
| Each time your heart beats, it squeezes blood into your | 72 |
| arteries. When this happens, the tubes bulge. The bulging | 81 |
| is called your pulse. When nurses hold your wrist, they feel | 92 |
| and count the bulges to find out how fast your heart is | 104 |
| beating. | 105 |
| You can feel your pulse in other places, too. Put your | 116 |
| index and middle fingers together, and then press them | 125 |
| gently on your neck, just below your chin. Count the | 135 |
| number of bulges, or beats, you feel in one minute. This | 146 |
| count tells you your heart rate, or the number of times | 157 |
| your heart beats in one minute. Your heart rate is lower | 168 |
| when you are resting. Worrying or exercising can increase | 177 |
| your heart rate. | 180 |

_____ /WCPM

# Oral Reading Fluency

| | |
|---|---|
| Last weekend we had a picnic in our neighborhood to | 10 |
| celebrate the end of summer. I saw one of our neighbors, a little | 23 |
| girl named Margaret. Margaret will start kindergarten in a few | 33 |
| days. I asked her whether she was excited about school. She | 44 |
| told me that she was, but she looked ready to cry. | 55 |
| I knew that she had gone to half-day preschool, so I said, | 67 |
| "You'll stay at school all day this year! Isn't that exciting?" | 78 |
| She nodded and walked away. I followed her over to her | 89 |
| mother, and I heard Margaret ask how long she'd stay in | 100 |
| kindergarten. Her mother said that she'd stay all day. | 109 |
| "So, will I miss dinner at home and will I get home when it's | 123 |
| dark outside?" Margaret asked with a brave face. | 131 |
| "Oh, no!" her mother responded. "You won't stay *all* day. | 141 |
| The bus will bring you home at 3 o'clock." | 150 |
| On the first day of school I saw Margaret on the bus. | 162 |
| "I didn't learn everything today," she said. "So they're | 171 |
| making me come back tomorrow." | 176 |
| Boy, does she have a lot to learn! | 184 |

# Oral Reading Fluency

| | |
|---|---:|
| A wolf is a member of the dog family. Unlike pet dogs, | 12 |
| wild wolves are not good companions for humans. They | 21 |
| are ferocious hunters. | 24 |
| Wolves live in groups called packs. Wolves in a pack | 34 |
| communicate with one another. One way they do this | 43 |
| is by howling. Many people think a wolf's howl is a | 54 |
| frightening sound. They often say wolves howl at the | 63 |
| moon. The truth is, wolves howl for different reasons. | 72 |
| A wolf might howl to tell the rest of the pack that they | 85 |
| should come together to start a hunt. Because wolves | 94 |
| hunt mostly at night, the moon happens to be out. A | 105 |
| wolf may howl to tell another animal to stay out of the | 117 |
| wolves' territory. If a wolf gets separated from the pack, it | 128 |
| may howl to tell the other pack members where it is. | 139 |
| Like our pet dogs, wolves also bark and growl. What | 149 |
| does it mean when a dog barks or growls? A wolf's bark | 161 |
| or growl might mean the same thing. A wolf uses these | 172 |
| sounds to say, "I'm angry!" | 177 |

_____ /WCPM

# Oral Reading Fluency

| | |
|---|---:|
| Today was rainy. Usually my sister and I complain to | 10 |
| our parents that we're bored. They usually come up with | 20 |
| a list of chores we could do so that we "won't be bored." | 33 |
| Well, that is not what happened today. | 40 |
| My sister and I were in her room complaining because | 50 |
| we wanted to play volleyball outside. My sister suggested | 59 |
| that we play inside. But, one of our main rules is that | 71 |
| there is to be no ball playing in the house. That rule came | 84 |
| after I broke a lamp with a softball. | 92 |
| We put our heads together and came up with a great | 103 |
| game using a balloon. We strung a piece of string across | 114 |
| the floor, just inches above the ground. We sat on the | 125 |
| floor, leaned back on our hands, and pushed up onto our | 136 |
| hands and feet. We would only be allowed to kick the | 147 |
| "ball" over the "net" with one foot. All three other limbs | 158 |
| had to stay on the floor. It was fun! So we invited two | 171 |
| friends over and had a great game of "foot-ball!" | 180 |

_____ /WCPM

# Oral Reading Fluency

Our solar system used to have nine planets. Now it has          11

eight. In August 2006, scientists decided that Pluto was          20

not a planet at all. Pluto is very small. It is even smaller          33

than our moon. Pluto is also very far away from Earth. It          45

is so small and so far away that it is hard to see, even with          60

a telescope. No space probe has ever gone there. As a          71

result, scientists know very little about Pluto.          78

Since Pluto was discovered in 1930, scientists have          86

wondered whether it really is a planet. This is partly          96

because it is so small and so far away. Now scientists have          108

decided to answer the question. First they had to answer          118

another question. What is a planet? They found that all          128

the other planets have at least three things in common.          138

Pluto has only two of these things. Scientists decided to          148

give Pluto a new title, "dwarf planet." Dwarf planets, like          158

the other planets, go around the sun. They also have a          169

nearly round shape.          172

Name _____

# Oral Reading Fluency

| | |
|---|---|
| If you have ever wished that you lived in a castle, keep | 12 |
| reading because you may soon change your mind! More | 21 |
| than a thousand years ago, royalty started constructing | 29 |
| stone castles because castles offered a safe place to live. | 39 |
| From the castle, people could protect their land from | 48 |
| enemies. Soldiers, servants, and animals lived inside the | 56 |
| castle making it a bustling, crowded place. | 63 |
| It was frequently damp and cold inside the walls of | 73 |
| stone castles. Even in the summer time, the stone rooms | 83 |
| remained damp causing people to spend as much time | 92 |
| outside the castle as possible. In the winter, cold winds | 102 |
| ripped through the rooms and hallways of a castle. | 111 |
| Rooms without a burning fire were quite cold. | 119 |
| Life in the castle was not very private because only | 129 |
| royalty had bedrooms and slept in beds. Most other | 138 |
| people slept in one large room called the great room on | 149 |
| benches or on the floor. Since most castles did not have | 160 |
| running water, people did not bathe every day. | 168 |
| Many castles remain standing today, but would you | 176 |
| want to live in one? | 181 |

_____ /WCPM

# Oral Reading Fluency

| | |
|---|---:|
| Bingwen raced to the bulletin board and searched it | 9 |
| for the cast list. He just knew that the music teacher had | 21 |
| picked him for the leading role in the play. He found his | 33 |
| name and ran his finger across the page to the list of | 45 |
| characters. Oh no! There must be a mistake. How could | 55 |
| he get such a small part? Bingwen read the list more | 66 |
| carefully. Leon, Bingwen's best friend, had received the | 74 |
| starring role. Leon hadn't even planned on trying out | 83 |
| until Bingwen had encouraged him to do so. | 91 |
| Bingwen decided that he wouldn't be in the play at all | 102 |
| if he couldn't be the star. | 108 |
| At lunch, Leon came up to Bingwen. Leon told | 117 |
| Bingwen that he felt bad. He wanted to drop out of the | 129 |
| play so that Bingwen could have the lead role. | 138 |
| At that moment, Bingwen realized that Leon was | 146 |
| willing to give up the lead just to make him happy. | 157 |
| Bingwen told Leon that he would make a great star and | 168 |
| that he couldn't wait to practice the play with him. | 178 |

# Oral Reading Fluency

| | |
|---|---:|
| For the last two years, Nadeem has tried to convince | **10** |
| his mother that he was responsible enough to have a | **20** |
| dog. When she agreed, Nadeem and Mom went to the | **30** |
| animal shelter. Nadeem knew that he wanted a puppy. | **39** |
| He was already planning the games they would play. | **48** |
| At the shelter, Nadeem heard barking and whining. He | **57** |
| thought some of the dogs sounded sad. Nadeem was | **66** |
| surprised to see the rows and rows of cages. Some dogs | **77** |
| whined in the back of their cages. Some dogs just wanted | **88** |
| to play. They wagged their tails and watched hopefully as | **98** |
| Nadeem walked past. | **101** |
| Nadeem looked at each dog. There were all shapes, | **110** |
| sizes, ages, and colors. Yet all the dogs had one thing in | **122** |
| common: they needed a home. | **127** |
| Nadeem turned to Mom. "I've made my decision," he | **136** |
| said. | **137** |
| "Already?" questioned Mom. "You haven't even taken | **144** |
| one dog out to play." | **149** |
| Nadeem decided that instead of taking home one dog, | **158** |
| he would come to the shelter after school each day. He | **169** |
| would be a volunteer and play with all of the dogs. | **180** |

# Oral Reading Fluency

|  |  |
|---|---|
| Lisa was trying to solve a mystery. Whenever she | 9 |
| bought cheese, it was gone within a few days. She had | 20 |
| no idea where it went. | 25 |
| "Perhaps I'm a sleepwalker, and I eat cheese in the | 35 |
| night," thought Lisa. | 38 |
| What Lisa did not know was that her cat, Louis, was | 49 |
| also a great lover of cheese. Louis's family came from | 59 |
| France. Cheese is very popular in France. Louis was also | 69 |
| fond of grapes and fine bread. These things were hard for | 80 |
| him to find in Lisa's house. | 86 |
| Louis made every effort to keep his habit a secret, but | 97 |
| Lisa discovered him eating a large piece of cheddar one | 107 |
| night when she got up to get a glass of water. | 118 |
| When Lisa turned on the light, she saw a piece of | 129 |
| cheese on the floor. She spotted crumbs in Louis's | 138 |
| whiskers. Louis was afraid that Lisa would be angry. | 147 |
| Instead, she reached down to pet the cat. "We solved the | 158 |
| cheese mystery!" she told Louis. He purred happily and | 167 |
| went back to finish the last bit of cheddar. | 176 |

# Oral Reading Fluency

| | |
|---|---|
| It was Denzel's first day working at the zoo, and | 10 |
| he was excited. Denzel's first task would be to follow | 20 |
| different workers around the zoo to learn about their | 29 |
| jobs. The first person he would work with was Melissa, | 39 |
| who worked in the reptile house—one of Denzel's most | 49 |
| favorite spots in the entire zoo. | 55 |
| Denzel and Melissa spent most of the morning | 63 |
| feeding the snakes. Denzel learned all the snakes' names | 72 |
| and which foods they best liked to eat. | 80 |
| When they got to the cage of Ike, the boa constrictor, | 91 |
| Melissa looked worried. Neither she nor Denzel could see | 100 |
| the snake. | 102 |
| "Oh no! Is Ike gone?" Melissa said. | 109 |
| Denzel looked through the glass and agreed that the | 118 |
| snake *did* seem to be missing. "Where on earth could he | 129 |
| be?" Denzel wondered aloud. Ike was awfully large to | 138 |
| have just disappeared. | 141 |
| Just then, something caught Denzel's eye—a flash of | 150 |
| brown under a log in the cage. "I think I've solved the | 162 |
| mystery," Denzel said, pointing to the well-hidden snake. | 170 |
| He and Melissa both breathed a sigh of relief. | 179 |

## Oral Reading Fluency

| | |
|---|---|
| Gus loved being a clown in the circus. He enjoyed | 10 |
| making children laugh. No one could make a better | 19 |
| balloon animal than Gus. Even though he loved his job, | 29 |
| Gus was looking forward to his vacation. He decided to | 39 |
| go to an amusement park on his first day off because he | 51 |
| loved riding roller coasters. | 55 |
| Gus woke up early so that he could try his favorite | 66 |
| rides before the lines became too long. At first, he was | 77 |
| very sleepy. But, as he entered the park gates, all the | 88 |
| sights and sounds of the amusement park woke him up. | 98 |
| Gus had a great time all day, yet he was puzzled by the | 111 |
| way some people acted. Children kept coming up to him | 121 |
| to ask for balloons. Could they somehow guess that he | 131 |
| was a clown, even though he was on vacation? | 140 |
| When he got home, Gus looked in a mirror for the first | 152 |
| time all day. He saw that he had gone to the park dressed | 165 |
| in his clown costume! His sleepiness that morning must | 174 |
| have caused him to put it on by accident! | 183 |

_____ /WCPM

# Oral Reading Fluency

| | |
|---|---|
| You may think that dragons live only in fairy tales. | **10** |
| Although there are no dragons that actually breathe fire | **19** |
| or fly, there are lizards in the real world that are called | **31** |
| Komodo dragons. | **33** |
| Komodo dragons can grow to be ten feet long and | **43** |
| can weigh up to 300 pounds. This makes them the | **53** |
| heaviest lizards on Earth. They have scaly skin; long, flat | **63** |
| heads; and strong, muscular tails. They have short legs | **72** |
| but can still run up to eleven miles per hour for short | **84** |
| periods of time. | **87** |
| Komodo dragons are skilled hunters. They use their | **95** |
| excellent sense of smell to help them find food. They also | **106** |
| use camouflage to hide from their prey. They use their | **116** |
| powerful jaws to eat deer, pigs, smaller dragons, and even | **126** |
| water buffalo. | **128** |
| Most Komodo dragons live in Indonesia. In America, | **136** |
| one of the only places to find Komodo dragons is in | **147** |
| zoos. Komodo dragons that live in zoos usually eat small | **157** |
| animals such as mice and rabbits. The giant lizards can | **167** |
| swallow these little animals whole. | **172** |

Name _____

# Oral Reading Fluency

| | |
|---|---|
| I've always known I wanted to be a dog detective. I | 11 |
| was strolling through the park one day, when WHAM! | 20 |
| I was knocked over by an enormous black dog. | 29 |
| "Hey!" I shouted, but the dog didn't stop. I looked | 39 |
| around for the dog's owner. When I didn't see anyone, I | 50 |
| took off after the dog. He raced down the path toward | 61 |
| the lake. I was running so fast after him that I slipped and | 74 |
| landed right in a mud puddle. | 80 |
| "He'll get away," I thought as I tried to wipe the mud | 92 |
| from my eyes. | 95 |
| I wasn't having much luck when, suddenly, I felt | 104 |
| something warm licking my face. The dog had come | 113 |
| back, and he was helping me. | 119 |
| His rough tongue tickled my nose and I started | 128 |
| laughing, even though my clothes were covered in mud. | 137 |
| I checked the dog's tags and realized that he was Mrs. | 148 |
| Davidson's dog Lucky who had been missing for over a | 158 |
| week. When she heard that I "captured" Lucky, she said | 168 |
| I was the best dog detective in the world! | 177 |

# Oral Reading Fluency

|  |  |
|---|---|
| Deserts are places on Earth that are very hot and dry. It | 12 |
| is difficult for most animals to survive in deserts. However, | 22 |
| some animals, such as camels, are made to live in deserts. | 33 |
| Camels can survive in the desert because they go | 42 |
| for long periods of time without drinking water. This is | 52 |
| helpful in the dry, dusty desert where water is hard to | 63 |
| find. When camels find water, they drink plenty of it. After | 74 |
| filling up, camels can go a week or more and not drink | 86 |
| another drop. | 88 |
| Camels have either one hump or two humps on their | 98 |
| backs. Some people think camels store water in their | 107 |
| humps, but camels really store food in their humps. | 116 |
| Because their bodies store food, camels can go months | 125 |
| between meals. This helps them survive in the desert | 134 |
| when they cannot find food for a long period of time. | 145 |
| Camels also do not seem to mind the hot weather | 155 |
| and desert sandstorms. They can withstand very high | 163 |
| temperatures without sweating. They have two rows | 170 |
| of long eyelashes to protect their eyes from desert | 179 |
| sandstorms. | 180 |

# Oral Reading Fluency

| | |
|---|---:|
| President Abraham Lincoln's youngest son was named | 7 |
| Thomas. Lincoln gave him the nickname "Tadpole" when | 15 |
| his son was born because the president thought Thomas | 24 |
| looked like a tadpole. Most people called the boy Tad. | 34 |
| Tad was very close to his father. | 41 |
| One year when Tad was ten, a turkey was sent to the | 53 |
| White House for the Lincoln family dinner during the | 62 |
| holidays. Tad named the turkey "Jack." He taught Jack to | 72 |
| follow him around the White House. When Tad found out | 82 |
| that the turkey was to be cooked for dinner, he was very | 94 |
| upset. | 95 |
| President Lincoln was in the middle of an important | 104 |
| meeting. Tad burst into the room, crying. He begged his | 114 |
| father to spare Jack's life. Lincoln thought carefully about | 123 |
| what to do. Then he took out a sheet of paper and wrote | 136 |
| an order. He wrote that Jack's life would be saved. | 146 |
| Since that day, the President spares a turkey's life | 155 |
| before every Thanksgiving Day. This is part of a long | 165 |
| tradition that began with Abraham Lincoln's son Tad. | 173 |

_____ /WCPM

# Oral Reading Fluency

| | |
|---|---|
| "Kimberly, are you ready? We don't want to be late to | 11 |
| meet the others," Kimberly's mother called to her. | 19 |
| Kimberly agreed that she didn't want to be late. They | 29 |
| were going camping with three other families from their | 38 |
| neighborhood. Kimberly had never been camping before, | 45 |
| but she knew that she would have fun because her three | 56 |
| best friends were going, too. | 61 |
| Yesterday, she and her friends had spent hours | 69 |
| planning their camping trip. Cameron was looking | 76 |
| forward to fishing in the lake. Kimberly wanted to fish, | 86 |
| too, but she didn't have a fishing pole. Cameron said that | 97 |
| he had an extra pole that she could borrow. | 106 |
| Nadia wanted to hike through the woods. She had | 115 |
| checked out a library book to help them identify different | 125 |
| animal tracks. Kimberly thought that sounded like fun. | 133 |
| Kelley had been camping last year. Her family had | 142 |
| taken a boat across the lake. Kimberly had never been on | 153 |
| a boat before, and she was excited about her first boat | 164 |
| trip. | 165 |
| As Kimberly raced down the hall, her dad asked, "Are | 175 |
| you ready?" | 177 |
| "Ready?" she asked. "I can hardly wait!" | 184 |

# Oral Reading Fluency

| | |
|---|---:|
| Cam did not enjoy her weekend chores. She wanted to | 10 |
| help around the house as her brother and sister did. Still, | 21 |
| she dreaded every Saturday morning. | 26 |
| Her mother let Cam try different chores each week, | 35 |
| hoping to find one that Cam might enjoy. First, Cam tried | 46 |
| laundry. After she turned her father's white work shirts | 55 |
| pink, her mother decided that Cam's older brother Mark | 64 |
| should probably keep doing the laundry. | 70 |
| Next, Cam tried vacuuming. She got a pair of socks | 80 |
| stuck in the vacuum cleaner by accident. Cam's sister, | 89 |
| Libby, took over after that. | 94 |
| Cam was sad. She felt that nothing she did helped her | 105 |
| family. | 106 |
| Then one Saturday morning, Cam's mother had an | 114 |
| idea. "Cam, why don't you help me weed the garden?" | 124 |
| Cam had never worked in the garden before, but she | 134 |
| liked being outside. She put on gardening gloves and | 143 |
| followed her mother outside. | 147 |
| After a few hours, Cam was still hard at work, but she | 159 |
| was enjoying herself. | 162 |
| "Cam, you did a great job!" her mother said happily. | 172 |
| "I think we have found the right chore for you." | 182 |

# Oral Reading Fluency

| | |
|---|---|
| When Clarence was in first grade, he was not happy. | 10 |
| "I am the shortest boy in my class, and it's terrible not | 22 |
| to be tall," Clarence used to say to his parents during | 33 |
| dinner. | 34 |
| When Clarence was in second grade, he WAS taller, | 43 |
| much taller. Now, though, he was upset because he could | 53 |
| not run as fast as the other kids. | 61 |
| "I am so slow. Everyone passes me when we run in | 72 |
| gym class, and it's awful to be slow," he used to tell his | 85 |
| mom and dad during dinner. | 90 |
| In third grade, Clarence could run faster. He found out, | 100 |
| though, that he was not a very good speller. | 109 |
| "I have a difficult time with spelling. I never do well on | 121 |
| spelling tests, and it's no fun being a terrible speller," he | 132 |
| said. | 133 |
| Now in fourth grade, Clarence is the tallest kid and the | 144 |
| fastest runner in his class. He is also the best speller in his | 157 |
| entire school. | 159 |
| "How do you feel now, Clarence?" his father asked. | 168 |
| "You mean about being tall and running and spelling? | 177 |
| It's no big deal," replied Clarence. | 183 |

**Oral Reading Fluency Recording Forms**

_____ /WCPM

# Oral Reading Fluency

| | |
|---|---|
| On a class trip to the seashore, Callie and Tina | 10 |
| searched for shells and rocks on the beach. Callie found | 20 |
| an old glass soda bottle in the sand. | 28 |
| "Look at this," Callie said as she picked up the bottle. | 39 |
| "There's something in it." | 43 |
| "Probably a worm," Tina said. | 48 |
| "No, it's a note," Callie replied, digging the muddy | 57 |
| paper out of the bottle. | 62 |
| "It says it's a map to an unbelievable treasure," Callie | 72 |
| explained. "'Go to the center of City Park and face away | 83 |
| from the sun. Take 200 long steps straight ahead and | 93 |
| then turn left and take 35 short steps. Climb the stairs. | 104 |
| Straight ahead, you will find great treasure.'" | 111 |
| The next Saturday, Callie and Tina asked Callie's | 119 |
| mother to take them to City Park. They excitedly followed | 129 |
| the directions in the note. After climbing the stairs, they | 139 |
| stopped suddenly, quite surprised. Before them was a | 147 |
| beautiful building. | 149 |
| "It's City Library," Callie's mother said. | 155 |
| "I've never been here," said Tina. | 161 |
| "The treasure must be in the things you can learn from | 172 |
| books," said Callie as she and Tina raced up the library's | 183 |
| steps. | 184 |

_____ /WCPM

## Oral Reading Fluency

| | |
|---|---:|
| What comes to mind when you think of a desert? | 10 |
| Do you see great hills of blowing sand? Do you imagine | 21 |
| camels with tall humps plodding slowly under a hot sun? | 31 |
| It's true that many deserts are sandy and hot. Deserts can | 42 |
| also be rocky, mountainous, or covered in snow and ice. | 52 |
|     A desert is an area that gets ten or fewer inches of | 64 |
| rain each year. Deserts cover about one-fifth of Earth's | 73 |
| surface. In most deserts, temperatures during the day | 81 |
| are extremely hot. At night, the desert air becomes very | 91 |
| cool. The exceptions are the deserts of Antarctica. These | 100 |
| deserts are cold all the time. | 106 |
|     The largest of all deserts is the Sahara in northern | 116 |
| Africa. The Sahara has mountains and sand dunes, but it | 126 |
| is mostly bare rock and gravel. Very few plants can grow | 137 |
| in the Sahara. In certain areas, people bring water from | 147 |
| faraway rivers. This helps them grow fruits, vegetables, | 155 |
| and grains. People raising herds of sheep and goats in the | 166 |
| desert often travel between their farms and the rivers. | 175 |

Name _____

## Selection Comprehension

▲ Choose the best answer for each question.

1. What is "Ruby the Copycat" MOST LIKE?

Ⓐ a fable

Ⓑ a fairy tale

Ⓒ realistic fiction

Ⓓ poetry

2. Why does Ruby say that she was a flower girl at her sister's wedding?

Ⓕ She wants to be just like Angela.

Ⓖ She is playing a game with Angela.

Ⓗ She knows her teacher likes weddings.

Ⓘ She is excited that she was in a wedding.

3. On Monday, Ruby's first day in class, how is Ruby different after she comes back from lunch?

Ⓐ She has on a sweater with daisies.

Ⓑ She is wearing a red bow in her hair.

Ⓒ She is wearing a hand-painted T-shirt.

Ⓓ She has on a red-and-lavender striped dress.

4. What is Ruby's BIGGEST problem in this story?

Ⓕ She tries to be like other people.

Ⓖ She does not like other people.

Ⓗ She never gets to have fun.

Ⓘ She is not good at reading.

**Selection Comprehension**
**"Ruby the Copycat"**
© Harcourt • Grade 3

5

## Written Response (worth two points)

READ
THINK
EXPLAIN

9. Explain how Angela's feelings toward Ruby change during the story. Use details and information from "Ruby the Copycat" to explain your answer.

Sample two-point response: At first, Angela is nice to Ruby and likes her. When she sees that Ruby is copying her all the time, she gets mad at Ruby and hurts her feelings. At the end of the story, they are friends again because Ruby stops copying.

7

**Selection Comprehension**
**"Ruby the Copycat"**
© Harcourt • Grade 3

TOTAL SCORE: _____ /8 + _____ /2

---

5. What happens JUST AFTER Angela writes a note to Ruby on Friday afternoon?
   - Ⓐ Ruby tiptoes to an empty desk.
   - Ⓑ Angela changes into a black dress.
   - Ⓒ The class cheers and claps their hands.
   - Ⓓ Miss Hart sends everyone home but Ruby.

6. What is the MOST important lesson Ruby learns in this story?
   - Ⓕ A true friend keeps your secrets.
   - Ⓖ It is important to just be yourself.
   - Ⓗ Time passes quickly if you are busy.
   - Ⓘ If you help others, they will help you.

7. What does Ruby do especially well?
   - Ⓐ draw
   - Ⓑ write
   - Ⓒ sing
   - Ⓓ hop

8. How does Ruby MOST LIKELY feel at the end of the story?
   - Ⓕ proud
   - Ⓖ angry
   - Ⓗ foolish
   - Ⓘ thoughtful

6

**Selection Comprehension**
**"Ruby the Copycat"**
© Harcourt • Grade 3

## Phonics/Spelling: Short Vowels

▲ Read each word. Then fill in the circle next to the word that has the same vowel sound and completes each sentence.

**1. tub**
The ____ is hungry.
- Ⓐ dog
- Ⓑ jug
- Ⓒ cat
- Ⓓ pup

**2. fresh**
There is a fish in our ____.
- Ⓕ net
- Ⓖ cast
- Ⓗ read
- Ⓘ brush

**3. magnet**
Wear your ____.
- Ⓐ candle
- Ⓑ socks
- Ⓒ hat
- Ⓓ mittens

**4. kitten**
Did you ____ the game?
- Ⓕ tag
- Ⓖ win
- Ⓗ lime
- Ⓘ stomp

Phonics/Spelling: Short Vowels /a/a,
/e/e, /i/i, /o/o, /u/u

8

TOTAL SCORE: _____ /4

---

## Focus Skill: Characters and Setting

▲ Read the passage. Then choose the best answer for each question.

### The Sand Worm

The Hernandez family was enjoying a day at the beach. It was almost time to go home. The sun was setting, and its light made the ocean shine. Anna's brother, George, showed her the shells he had found. He looked at her sand sculpture.

"Wow!" he said. "That looks just like a crocodile!"

"That's right," Anna said, grinning. "I wanted to make a scary sand crocodile going into the ocean."

As the children talked, the waves came closer and closer to the sand crocodile.

"Oh, no!" said Anna.

*Crash! Swish!* A wave washed away the crocodile's long mouth. *Crash! Swish!* Another wave washed away the crocodile's front legs. Soon only its tail was left.

"I'm so sorry," said George.

"It's okay," said Anna, laughing. "Now it looks like a funny worm going into the ocean!"

1. What is the setting of the story?
- Ⓐ a lake
- Ⓑ a beach
- Ⓒ a river
- Ⓓ a garden

Focus Skill: Characters and Setting

9

---

Name _____

# Use Alphabetical Order

▲ **Choose the best answer for each question.**

1. Which word would come first in alphabetical order?

   Ⓐ slip
   Ⓑ song
   Ⓒ sick
   Ⓓ smell

2. Which word would appear on the dictionary page that has the guide words *desk* and *dish* at the top?

   Ⓕ dig
   Ⓖ dance
   Ⓗ drum
   Ⓘ duck

3. Where does the word *trip* belong?

   table    tonight    turn    twelve

   Ⓐ before *table*
   Ⓑ between *tonight* and *turn*
   Ⓒ between *turn* and *twelve*
   Ⓓ after *twelve*

4. What guide words would be at the top of the dictionary page where *pitcher* appears?

   Ⓕ plant, pond
   Ⓖ patch, penny
   Ⓗ phone, place
   Ⓘ present, puppet

Use Alphabetical Order

© Harcourt • Grade 3

11

TOTAL SCORE: _____ /4

---

Name _____

2. At what time of day does the story take place?

   Ⓕ morning
   Ⓖ noon
   Ⓗ afternoon
   Ⓘ midnight

3. Which word describes Anna?

   Ⓐ cheerful
   Ⓑ angry
   Ⓒ shy
   Ⓓ funny

4. How do you know that George is kind?

   Ⓕ He collects shells when he goes to the beach.
   Ⓖ He is sorry that the waves washed the crocodile away.
   Ⓗ He tells funny jokes to make his sister laugh.
   Ⓘ He helps Anna make another sand crocodile.

Focus Skill: Characters and Setting

© Harcourt • Grade 3

10

TOTAL SCORE: _____ /4

# Robust Vocabulary

▲ Choose the word that best completes each sentence.

**1.** I couldn't hear the secret she _____ to her friend.
- Ⓐ modeled
- Ⓑ gushed
- Ⓒ murmured
- Ⓓ recited

**2.** Having the same kind of dog for a pet is a funny _____.
- Ⓕ itinerary
- Ⓖ coincidence
- Ⓗ contact
- Ⓘ enthusiast

**3.** Dogs are known to be _____ to their owners.
- Ⓐ inexplicable
- Ⓑ pleasant
- Ⓒ bizarre
- Ⓓ loyal

**4.** The teacher _____ how to solve the math problem.
- Ⓕ modeled
- Ⓖ gushed
- Ⓗ recited
- Ⓘ murmured

**5.** The weather on warm spring days is very _____.
- Ⓐ loyal
- Ⓑ chilly
- Ⓒ bizarre
- Ⓓ pleasant

**6.** We proudly _____ the Pledge of Allegiance before the game.
- Ⓕ imitated
- Ⓖ modeled
- Ⓗ recited
- Ⓘ murmured

**7.** We _____ through the snow to get to the cabin.
- Ⓐ frustrated
- Ⓑ trudged
- Ⓒ murmured
- Ⓓ imitated

**8.** The parrot _____ my words exactly.
- Ⓕ squatted
- Ⓖ trudged
- Ⓗ imitated
- Ⓘ gushed

**9.** Waiting in line makes me feel _____.
- Ⓐ trudged
- Ⓑ recited
- Ⓒ gushed
- Ⓓ frustrated

**10.** She _____, "That kitten is so cute!"
- Ⓕ gushed
- Ⓖ imitated
- Ⓗ recited
- Ⓘ modeled

TOTAL SCORE: _____ /10

## Oral Reading Fluency

Once upon a time there was a greedy dog. Even 10

though he had plenty of food and toys, he always desired 21

more. One afternoon he observed a little puppy chewing 30

on a huge bone. 34

"Give me that bone," the greedy dog growled. The 43

frightened puppy dropped the bone and scurried away. 51

The greedy dog scooped up the bone and marched on 61

his way. 63

As the greedy dog crossed a bridge over a creek, he 74

glanced over the edge of the bridge and noticed another 84

dog staring up at him from the water. That dog also had 96

a huge bone in his mouth. The greedy dog decided he 107

wanted that bone, too. 111

He bared his teeth and let out a fierce growl. Much 122

to his disbelief, the dog in the water growled back. The 133

greedy dog snapped at the bone in the other dog's 143

mouth. Plop! The bone in the greedy dog's mouth fell 153

into the water, and the other dog vanished. 161

"That dog has stolen my bone!" thought the greedy 170

dog. "I must find him!" 175

Of course, he never did. 180

**Oral Reading Fluency**

15

_____ /WCPM

---

## Grammar: Sentences: Statements and Questions

▲ **Choose the best answer for each question.**

1. Which sentence is written correctly?
   - Ⓐ otters swim very well.
   - Ⓑ Are otters mammals
   - Ⓒ The otter has brown fur
   - Ⓓ An otter eats fish.

2. Which sentence is written correctly?
   - Ⓕ Bananas are my favorite fruit.
   - Ⓖ That lemon is sour
   - Ⓗ Do you like oranges
   - Ⓘ there is an apple tree in the yard.

3. Which sentence is a statement?
   - Ⓐ Is it snowing?
   - Ⓑ I have my coat.
   - Ⓒ May I go outside?
   - Ⓓ Where is the car.

4. Which sentence is a question?
   - Ⓕ Did you clean your room?
   - Ⓖ Your room is a mess.
   - Ⓗ Put your toys away.
   - Ⓘ I will help you.

**Grammar: Sentences: Statements and Questions**

14

TOTAL SCORE: _____ /4

Name _____

## Selection Comprehension

▲ Choose the best answer for each question.

1. Where does the story take place?
   - Ⓐ at Eddie's home
   - Ⓑ at Eddie's school
   - Ⓒ at Mrs. Morrow's house
   - Ⓓ at a famous writer's office

2. Which sentence BEST tells what the story is about?
   - Ⓕ Eddie reads ten books by one writer.
   - Ⓖ Eddie chooses a title for a new story.
   - Ⓗ Eddie meets a real author at his school.
   - Ⓘ Eddie gets to decorate the school hallway.

3. What is Eddie's BIGGEST problem in the story?
   - Ⓐ He wants to know how authors know what to write.
   - Ⓑ He cannot think of enough "Ideas to Write About."
   - Ⓒ He worries the visiting author will not like his story.
   - Ⓓ He is afraid the other children are better writers than he is.

4. What does the "real author" say is the best way to become a writer?
   - Ⓕ have exciting adventures
   - Ⓖ study hard in school
   - Ⓗ read a lot of books
   - Ⓘ tell stories to friends

Name _____

5. How does Eddie MOST LIKELY feel when he does not get to ask his important question?
   - Ⓐ brave
   - Ⓑ cheerful
   - Ⓒ frightened
   - Ⓓ disappointed

6. With which idea would the author of the story MOST LIKELY agree?
   - Ⓕ Writing is difficult work.
   - Ⓖ Everyone has a story to tell.
   - Ⓗ Anyone can become famous.
   - Ⓘ Stories should have surprise endings.

7. How can readers tell that "The Day Eddie Met the Author" is realistic fiction?
   - Ⓐ It has animals that act like people act.
   - Ⓑ It tells about an American folk hero.
   - Ⓒ It happens at a real time and place long ago.
   - Ⓓ It has characters with feelings that real people have.

8. What is Eddie MOST LIKELY to tell at the end of his new story?
   - Ⓕ that he learned he could be a writer
   - Ⓖ what kind of books are his favorites
   - Ⓗ how he prepared for the author's visit
   - Ⓘ which other famous writers he has met

## Phonics/Spelling: Root Words and Endings

▲ Choose the word that correctly completes each sentence.

1. Yesterday we _____ for a new pair of shoes.
   - (A) shop
   - (B) shops
   - (C) shopped
   - (D) shopping

2. The clown _____ in a circle.
   - (F) danced
   - (G) dances
   - (H) dancing
   - (I) dance

3. She is _____ a flower.
   - (A) plants
   - (B) plant
   - (C) planted
   - (D) planting

4. Max _____ in New York until he was three.
   - (F) live
   - (G) lived
   - (H) lives
   - (I) living

Phonics/Spelling: Root Words and
Endings: *-ed, -ing*
© Harcourt • Grade 3

19

TOTAL SCORE: _____ /4

---

READ
THINK
EXPLAIN

## Written Response (worth two points)

9. **COMPARING TEXTS** Eddie in "The Day Eddie Met the Author" and the narrator in "Surprise" both wonder about the same thing when they read books. Explain what BOTH Eddie and the narrator wonder about when they read. Use information from the story and the poem to explain your answer.

**Sample two-point response: Both Eddie and the narrator**

**feel like book authors write parts that are just for them.**

**They wonder how the writers know how to write special**

**parts for each reader.**

Selection Comprehension
"The Day Eddie Met the Author"
© Harcourt • Grade 3

18

TOTAL SCORE: _____ /8 + _____ /2

---

Name _____

## Focus Skill: Characters and Setting

▲ Read the passage. Then choose the best answer for each question.

### Presents in the Sky

Kim and Lia heard their mother calling. Lia slowed the swing and jumped off. Kim walked over from the slide.

"The sky is getting dark. The fireworks will begin soon," said Kim. "Let's go!"

Kim and Lia ran to the blanket their mother had spread on the grass. All around them, families waited for darkness.

Suddenly, a loud boom startled everyone. Bright lights lit up the sky. Lia covered her ears and began to cry. Kim put her arm around her sister as more fireworks lit the sky.

"This is a special night, Lia," said Kim. "It's July Fourth. We are Americans now. Tonight the whole country has a birthday party. These lights are the presents. Look how pretty they are!"

Lia moved her hands away from her ears. She held hands with her sister and her mother. They watched the rest of the fireworks show.

"Happy birthday, America," Lia said with a smile.

1. What is the setting of the story?

   Ⓐ a home
   Ⓑ a school
   Ⓒ a park
   Ⓓ a restaurant

Focus Skill: Characters and Setting

© Harcourt • Grade 3

20

---

Name _____

2. At what time of day does the story take place?

   Ⓕ morning
   Ⓖ noon
   Ⓗ afternoon
   Ⓘ night

3. How do you know Lia is scared?

   Ⓐ She covers her ears and cries.
   Ⓑ She holds hands with Kim.
   Ⓒ She gets off the swing.
   Ⓓ She says, "Happy birthday."

4. Which word describes Kim?

   Ⓕ worried
   Ⓖ selfish
   Ⓗ afraid
   Ⓘ caring

Focus Skill: Characters and Setting

© Harcourt • Grade 3

21

TOTAL SCORE: _____ /4

Name _____

## Robust Vocabulary

▲ Choose the word that best completes each sentence.

1. Only the teacher can _____ you from class.
   - (A) dismiss
   - (B) conquer
   - (C) ponder
   - (D) model

2. We say the Pledge of Allegiance at the start of every _____.
   - (F) anticipation
   - (G) coincidence
   - (H) resistance
   - (I) assembly

3. The puppy _____ to get out of the boy's arms.
   - (A) pondered
   - (B) dismissed
   - (C) squirmed
   - (D) autographed

4. The students used scraps to make a _____ floor pillow.
   - (F) loyal
   - (G) patchwork
   - (H) pleasant
   - (I) frustrated

5. The famous basketball player _____ my ticket.
   - (A) autographed
   - (B) dismissed
   - (C) pondered
   - (D) squirmed

Robust Vocabulary

© Harcourt • Grade 3

23

---

Name _____

## Use Alphabetical Order

▲ Choose the best answer for each question.

1. Which word comes first in alphabetical order?
   - (A) branch
   - (B) basket
   - (C) bush
   - (D) block

2. Which group of words is in alphabetical order?
   - (F) path, pencil, price, play
   - (G) pay, puppy, purple, pen
   - (H) peek, people, pink, plum
   - (I) pig, plate, past, power

3. Where does the word *drive* belong?

   dollar   draw   drum   dust

   - (A) before *dollar*
   - (B) between *dollar* and *draw*
   - (C) between *draw* and *drum*
   - (D) between *drum* and *dust*

4. Which guide words would be at the top of the dictionary page where the word *storm* appears?
   - (F) sleep, soup
   - (G) spin, stage
   - (H) strong, summer
   - (I) stick, stretch

Use Alphabetical Order

© Harcourt • Grade 3

22

TOTAL SCORE: _____ /4

Weekly
Lesson Test
Lesson 2

## Grammar: Commands and Exclamations

▲ Choose the best answer for each question.

1. Which sentence is a command?
   - (A) Sit down, please.
   - (B) Where is my seat?
   - (C) I sit behind Mark.
   - (D) Who sits near you?

2. Which sentence is an exclamation?
   - (F) We went to the bookstore.
   - (G) May I buy a new book?
   - (H) My favorite author signed my book!
   - (I) Read a good book every week.

3. Which sentence is written correctly?
   - (A) I have a new pet?
   - (B) Feed the kitten.
   - (C) Stop scratching the chair?
   - (D) Have you seen my kitten.

4. Which sentence is written correctly?
   - (F) I like soccer and basketball?.
   - (G) May I play outside.
   - (H) I'm going outside to play soccer?
   - (I) Get out of the street!

TOTAL SCORE: _____ /4

---

Weekly
Lesson Test
Lesson 2

6. There are many toys and puzzles, so you will have _____ to do.
   - (F) anticipation
   - (G) resistance
   - (H) assembly
   - (I) plenty

7. I know I can _____ my fear of the dark.
   - (A) murmur
   - (B) imitate
   - (C) ponder
   - (D) conquer

8. I need time to _____ what the story means.
   - (F) recite
   - (G) ponder
   - (H) dismiss
   - (I) conquer

9. She waited with _____ for the day of the party.
   - (A) anticipation
   - (B) plenty
   - (C) resistance
   - (D) patchwork

10. He felt _____ to an earlier bedtime.
   - (F) plenty
   - (G) assembly
   - (H) coincidence
   - (I) resistance

TOTAL SCORE: _____ /10

---

Name _____

## Oral Reading Fluency

Dylan was eager to begin his first camping trip. His 10
parents had packed the tent and sleeping bags in the car. 21
Dylan had borrowed a book about camping from 29
the library. He began to read the book during the trip in 41
the car. Dylan was very interested in the chapter titled 51
"Camping Safely." He carefully read the page about 59
poison ivy. 61

"The leaves grow in groups of three," Dylan read 70
aloud. "Study the picture of this poisonous plant on the 80
next page." But, someone had torn out the page with 90
the picture of the plant! 95

That afternoon, the family went for a walk in the 105
woods. Dylan counted the leaves on each plant they 114
passed. Suddenly, his brother pointed at an owl sitting 123
in a tree. Dylan forgot the plants as he stepped closer to 135
the tree. 137

"Dylan," said his mother, "you're standing in poison 145
ivy! Get out of there!" 150

Dylan looked down and counted the leaves, "One, 158
two, and three." Realizing his mistake, he turned and 167
ran back to the trail. 172

"Well, now you know what poison ivy looks like!" said 182
his dad. 184

_____ /WCPM

Oral Reading Fluency
© Harcourt • Grade 3

`26`

Name _____

## Selection Comprehension

► Choose the best answer for each question.

1. Why did the author write "Schools Around the World"?

    Ⓐ to tell about different kinds of schools
    Ⓑ to describe one special kind of school
    Ⓒ to prove which kind of school is best
    Ⓓ to tell what schools were like long ago

2. Based on the passage, what can readers tell about schools around the world?

    Ⓕ They are the same size.
    Ⓖ They have many holidays.
    Ⓗ They are open only part of the day.
    Ⓘ They bring teachers and learners together.

3. Why does the author write words under some pictures?

    Ⓐ to tell who took the picture
    Ⓑ to repeat ideas in smaller print
    Ⓒ to explain what the picture shows
    Ⓓ to ask questions the reader should answer

4. The passage says that some children go to a boarding school when they need to

    Ⓕ live away from home.
    Ⓖ study math and science.
    Ⓗ help their family earn money.
    Ⓘ study more than one language.

Selection Comprehension
"Schools Around the World"
© Harcourt • Grade 3

`27`

Name _____

## Written Response (worth two points)

READ
THINK
EXPLAIN

9. If you could go to one of the schools described in the passage, which kind of school would you choose? Tell which kind of school you would go to, and explain why you would like to go there. Use information and details from "Schools Around the World" to help you explain your answer.

Sample two-point response: I would like to go to a school

that doesn't have walls. I would like to sit outside and

see trees and mountains while I learn. I would also like

to go where I could learn to dance.

29

Selection Comprehension
"Schools Around the World"
© Harcourt • Grade 3

TOTAL SCORE: _____ /8 + _____ /2

---

Name _____

5. Under which heading would the author be MOST LIKELY to add a picture of children riding horses to school?

Ⓐ School Clothing
Ⓑ School Buildings
Ⓒ Getting to School
Ⓓ Learning to Read and Write

6. How is what children learn the SAME in different countries?

Ⓕ They all learn two different languages.
Ⓖ They all learn to use computers.
Ⓗ They all learn art and music.
Ⓘ They all learn new ideas.

7. Which would MOST help you understand the ideas in this passage?

Ⓐ reading the titles of your school books
Ⓑ picturing in your mind the schools described
Ⓒ asking a teacher how your school got its name
Ⓓ remembering the first day you went to school

8. How can readers tell that "Schools Around the World" is expository nonfiction?

Ⓕ It tells about the life of an important person.
Ⓖ It gives facts and information about a subject.
Ⓗ It has a plot with a beginning, middle, and ending.
Ⓘ It has story events that could not happen in real life.

28

Selection Comprehension
"Schools Around the World"
© Harcourt • Grade 3

---

*Student Edition* pp. 28–29

45

© Harcourt • Grade 3

Name _____

## Phonics/Spelling: Vowel Digraphs

▲ Read each word. Then fill in the circle under the word that has the same vowel sound and completes each sentence.

**1. rain**

I like to _____ when I get home from school.

- Ⓐ call
- Ⓑ snack
- Ⓒ play
- Ⓓ clean

**2. heat**

I laughed at the _____ in the show.

- Ⓕ bear
- Ⓖ seal
- Ⓗ men
- Ⓘ clown

**3. toast**

There's a big _____ on the gift.

- Ⓐ name
- Ⓑ toy
- Ⓒ tag
- Ⓓ bow

**4. green**

Are there fish in the _____?

- Ⓕ stream
- Ⓖ lake
- Ⓗ wreck
- Ⓘ well

**Phonics/Spelling: Vowel Digraphs: ee, ea; ai, ay; oa, ow**
© Harcourt • Grade 3

`30`

TOTAL SCORE: _____ /4

---

Name _____

## Focus Skill: Locate Information

▲ Read the passage. Then choose the best answer for each question.

### It Came from Mexico

In the United States, we enjoy many things that come from Mexico.

#### Food

Almost 2,000 years ago, people in Mexico were making chocolate. So many people valued it that it was used as money! You have probably eaten a taco or a tortilla. Both of these foods come from Mexico.

#### Animals

Orange and black monarch butterflies are easy to spot. Each spring, millions of these insects travel about 3,000 miles from Mexico to the United States.

The Chihuahua, a tiny dog, comes from Mexico.

#### Toys

You may have been at a party and hit a piñata with a stick. What did the piñata look like? Was there candy inside? The piñata comes from Mexico.

**Focus Skill: Locate Information**
© Harcourt • Grade 3

`31`

---

## Use a Dictionary

▲ Read the dictionary entry. Then choose the best answer for each question.

**guide** words: *head, heel*

**head** (hed) *n.* **1.** The topmost part of the body. **2.** A single animal. *The rancher had 200 head of cattle.* **3.** A person who leads or is in charge. **4.** The leading position. *The mayor was at the head of the parade.*
*v.* **1.** To be in charge of; lead. **2.** To aim, point, or turn in a certain direction.

**heal** (hēl) *v.* **1.** To make a person well. **2.** To be repaired naturally. *His bruise healed in two weeks.*

**health** (helth) *n.* The overall condition of a living thing.

**heap** (hēp) *n.* A group of things placed or thrown, one on top of the other.
*v.* To throw or pile things, one on top of the other.

**hear** (hir) *v.* **heard** (hûrd), **hear•ing** To sense sounds with the ear.

**heat** (hēt) *n.* **1.** The transfer of energy felt as an increase in temperature. **2.** One round in a competition, such as a race.
*v.* To make warm or hot.

Use a Dictionary
© Harcourt • Grade 3

33

---

1. In which section would you expect to find facts about the Bolson tortoise, which comes from Mexico?
   - Ⓐ Introduction
   - Ⓑ Food
   - Ⓒ Animals
   - Ⓓ Toys

2. This is the table of contents for this book. Which chapter would you read to learn about the flag of Mexico?

   - Ⓕ Chapter 1: The Geography of Mexico
   - Ⓖ Chapter 2: The History of Mexico
   - Ⓗ Chapter 3: The People of Mexico
   - Ⓘ Chapter 4: The Symbols of Mexico

3. What information does the caption give?
   - Ⓐ the number of dogs in the United States
   - Ⓑ directions on how to care for a dog
   - Ⓒ the name of a dog that comes from Mexico
   - Ⓓ the year that dogs first came to the United States

4. Where would you look to find the author of this book?
   - Ⓕ title page
   - Ⓖ table of contents
   - Ⓗ glossary
   - Ⓘ index

Focus Skill: Locate Information
© Harcourt • Grade 3

32

TOTAL SCORE: _____ /4

Name _____

# Robust Vocabulary

▲ **Choose the word that best completes each sentence.**

1. I earn money if I do extra _____ at home.
   - (A) assemblies
   - (B) chores ●
   - (C) resources
   - (D) uniforms

2. You can use library _____ to write the report.
   - (F) uniforms
   - (G) coincidences
   - (H) chores
   - (I) resources ●

3. Are you _____ that your homework is in your backpack?
   - (A) certain ●
   - (B) diverse
   - (C) loyal
   - (D) proper

4. Do the students at your school wear _____?
   - (F) chores
   - (G) uniforms ●
   - (H) patchwork
   - (I) resources

5. We studied the _____ of Mexico.
   - (A) tutor
   - (B) chores
   - (C) culture ●
   - (D) assembly

Robust Vocabulary

---

Name _____

1. What are the guide words on this dictionary page?
   - (A) *head* and *heat*
   - (B) *heal* and *heel*
   - (C) *head* and *heel* ●
   - (D) *hear* and *heat*

2. Which entry is after *hear*?
   - (F) heal
   - (G) heap
   - (H) heat ●
   - (I) health

3. Which definition of *head* is used in the sentence below?

   **My mom will *head* the meeting at school.**
   - (A) *n.* The topmost part of the body
   - (B) *n.* A single animal
   - (C) *v.* To be in charge of; lead ●
   - (D) *v.* To aim, point, or turn in a certain direction

4. **heat** (hēt) *n.* **1.** The transfer of energy felt as an increase in temperature. **2.** One round in a competition, such as a race.
   *v.* To make warm or hot.

   Which sentence could appear in the dictionary for the last definition of *heat*?
   - (F) She swam in the second heat.
   - (G) I feel the heat coming from the oven.
   - (H) If you are too warm, I can turn down the heat.
   - (I) I can heat the sticks by rubbing them together. ●

   TOTAL SCORE: _____ /4

Use a Dictionary

---

***Student Edition*** pp. 34–35

## Grammar: Complete and Simple Subjects and Predicates

▲ **Choose the best answer for each question.**

1. What is the complete subject in this sentence?

   **The colorful flowers bloomed all spring.**

   Ⓐ bloomed

   Ⓑ colorful flowers

   Ⓒ The colorful flowers

   Ⓓ bloomed all spring

2. What is the complete predicate in this sentence?

   **The lost puppy followed me home.**

   Ⓕ puppy

   Ⓖ followed

   Ⓗ The lost puppy

   Ⓘ followed me home

3. What is the simple subject in this sentence?

   **The dark-green frog jumped into the pond.**

   Ⓐ frog

   Ⓑ The dark-green frog

   Ⓒ jumped

   Ⓓ jumped into the pond

4. What is the simple predicate in this sentence?

   **Bright red apples grow on the tree.**

   Ⓕ Bright red apples

   Ⓖ apples

   Ⓗ grow

   Ⓘ apples grow

Grammar: Complete and Simple
Subjects and Predicates
© Harcourt • Grade 3

`37`

TOTAL SCORE: _____ /4

---

6. The _____ helps me understand math.

   Ⓕ tutor

   Ⓖ culture

   Ⓗ assembly

   Ⓘ literacy

7. A good education focuses on _____ .

   Ⓐ resources

   Ⓑ boarding

   Ⓒ literacy

   Ⓓ anticipation

8. A _____ classroom has a computer and references for the teacher.

   Ⓕ loyal

   Ⓖ certain

   Ⓗ proper

   Ⓘ diverse

9. The committee members were a _____ group, including a teacher, a scientist, and an actor.

   Ⓐ diverse

   Ⓑ loyal

   Ⓒ proper

   Ⓓ certain

10. This year, Mr. Smyth is _____ his horses at Circle Q Stables.

    Ⓕ pondering

    Ⓖ conquering

    Ⓗ dismissing

    Ⓘ boarding

**Robust Vocabulary**
© Harcourt • Grade 3

`36`

TOTAL SCORE: _____ /10

Name _____

## Selection Comprehension

▲ Choose the best answer for each question.

**1.** What is "Ellen Ochoa, Astronaut" MOST LIKE?
Ⓐ a tall tale
Ⓑ a mystery
Ⓒ a fairy tale
Ⓓ a biography

**2.** Ellen's mother told her to "reach for the stars" because she
wanted Ellen to
Ⓕ explore space.
Ⓖ become a pilot.
Ⓗ follow her dreams.
Ⓘ learn more about science.

**3.** What was special about Ellen's flight into space?
Ⓐ She invented a robot while in flight.
Ⓑ She made the first flight to a space station.
Ⓒ She was the first Hispanic woman in space.
Ⓓ She stayed in flight longer than anyone else.

**4.** Which happened AFTER Ellen flew on the space shuttle
*Discovery?*
Ⓕ Ellen delivered supplies to other astronauts.
Ⓖ Ellen joined a space research center.
Ⓗ Ellen got a job as an engineer.
Ⓘ Ellen learned to fly a plane.

**Selection Comprehension**
**"Ellen Ochoa, Astronaut"**
© Harcourt • Grade 3

**39**

---

Name _____

## Oral Reading Fluency

| | |
|---|---:|
| Alex froze when he saw the clown walk into the yard. | 11 |
| He couldn't let his friends at the party know that he was | 23 |
| terrified of clowns! | 26 |
| Alex joined the group of kids who had gathered | 35 |
| around the clown. "It's just a clown," he whispered | 44 |
| to himself. | 46 |
| From behind, Alex heard someone say, "It's just a | 55 |
| clown." Worried that someone was making fun of him, | 64 |
| Alex slowly turned around. He saw a five-year-old boy, | 73 |
| sobbing quietly while his mother tried to comfort him. | 82 |
| "I think I can help," Alex said to the boy's mother. | 93 |
| She smiled gratefully and stepped aside. He bent and | 102 |
| whispered in the boy's ear. "When I was a kid," he said, | 115 |
| "I was afraid of clowns, too." | 120 |
| "You're not afraid of them now? They're so scary!" | 130 |
| the boy said. | 132 |
| "I faced my fear," Alex said. "Look at that clown. He's | 143 |
| really pretty silly if you watch him." | 150 |
| Alex and the boy watched the clown for a little while, | 161 |
| and then the boy chuckled. Alex was happy to know that | 172 |
| by helping someone else, he had learned to control his | 182 |
| own fear. | 184 |

**Oral Reading Fluency**
© Harcourt • Grade 3

**38**

_____ /WCPM

---

Name _____

**Written Response** (worth two points)

READ
THINK
EXPLAIN

9. Why was Ellen good at so many things? Use information and details from "Ellen Ochoa, Astronaut" to support your answer.

Sample two-point response: Ellen always worked hard

to get ahead. She was determined to do her best and

wouldn't give up. She also did things she loved.

_____

_____

41

**Selection Comprehension**
"Ellen Ochoa, Astronaut"
© Harcourt • Grade 3

TOTAL SCORE: _____ /8 + _____ /2

---

Name _____

5. Readers can tell that Ellen is

Ⓐ shy.

Ⓑ gentle.

Ⓒ lonely.

Ⓓ determined.

6. Why does the author tell that Ellen failed to get into the space program in 1985?

Ⓕ to show that Ellen did not give up

Ⓖ to make readers feel happy for Ellen

Ⓗ to show that Ellen had not worked hard

Ⓘ to make readers upset about how Ellen was treated

7. Under which heading should readers look to find out about Ellen's flight on the space shuttle *Discovery?*

Ⓐ "The Early Years"

Ⓑ "A Trip into Space"

Ⓒ "Astronaut Training"

Ⓓ "Inventor and Musician"

8. Why did the author write "Ellen Ochoa, Astronaut"?

Ⓕ to teach how to become an astronaut

Ⓖ to tell about one very special astronaut

Ⓗ to tell a funny story about an astronaut

Ⓘ to explain why astronauts are important

40

**Selection Comprehension**
"Ellen Ochoa, Astronaut"
© Harcourt • Grade 3

---

*Student Edition pp. 40–41*

© Harcourt • Grade 3

Name _____

## Phonics/Spelling: Plurals -s, -es

▲ Choose the word that correctly completes each sentence.

1. We looked for the book in three different ___.

   Ⓐ store
   Ⓑ stores
   Ⓒ stories
   Ⓓ stors

2. The third graders planted ___ in the schoolyard.

   Ⓕ daisy
   Ⓖ daisys
   Ⓗ daisyes
   Ⓘ daisies

3. Do you wear ___ when you read?

   Ⓐ glass
   Ⓑ glassies
   Ⓒ glasses
   Ⓓ glass's

4. My ___ were cold when I marched in the parade.

   Ⓕ hands
   Ⓖ handes
   Ⓗ handies
   Ⓘ handy

Phonics/Spelling: Plurals -s, -es

© Harcourt • Grade 3

42

---

Name _____

## Focus Skill: Locate Information

▲ Read the passage. Then choose the best answer for each question.

### Amazing Dogs

Many people believe that dogs are people's best friends. In addition to being great pets, dogs can do some amazing things.

**Wuffy**

Most dogs chase cats, but not Wuffy! She rescues them. Wuffy has rescued more than 200 cats. She takes care of lost kittens as if they were her own. Wuffy also takes care of sick cats and kittens.

**Faith**

Faith was born without her front two legs. A boy rescued her when she was very young. At first, she could only drag herself across the floor. Slowly, her family taught her to walk on her back legs—just like a human.

**Sabrina**

Do you like to ride a skateboard? Sabrina does! Sabrina is a bulldog that loves to ride a skateboard. It's a trick that she taught herself. Sabrina pushes the skateboard until it's rolling. Then, she hops on and rides. Her owner says Sabrina would ride all day. "Sometimes we have to hide it," her owner says.

1. How did the author choose the headings?

   Ⓐ The headings each name a different kind of pet.
   Ⓑ Each heading is the name of a dog.
   Ⓒ Each heading describes what an animal can do.
   Ⓓ The headings are in alphabetical order.

Focus Skill: Locate Information

© Harcourt • Grade 3

43

TOTAL SCORE: ___ /4

Name _____

## Use a Dictionary

▶ Read the dictionary entries. Choose the best answer for each question.

*road*        *robot*

**road** (rōd) *n.* 1. A route for vehicles to drive on, a street. 2. A course or path. *The road to riches.*

**roam** (rōm) *v.* **roamed, roam•ing, roams** To move about without a plan; wander.

**roar** (rôr) *v.* **roared, roar•ing, roars** 1. To make a loud, deep growling noise. *I heard the lion roar.* 2. To laugh or cheer loudly or excitedly. 3. To shout. *n.* 1. The loud, deep cry of a wild animal. *The lion's roar is loud.* 2. A loud noise made by something burning. *The roar of the fire was loud.* 3. A loud burst of laughter.

**robot** (rō′bot) *n.* A machine that can be programmed to do tasks.

1. What are the guide words on this dictionary page?

  Ⓐ *road* and *robot*

  Ⓑ *road* and *roam*

  Ⓒ *road* and *rock*

  Ⓓ *roar* and *robot*

Use a Dictionary      45

© Harcourt • Grade 3

---

Name _____

2. This is the Table of Contents for this book. In which chapter would you expect to find information about animals that live in the sea?

    **Chapter 1: Cat Tales**      1

    **Chapter 2: Amazing Dogs**    10

    **Chapter 3: In the Water**      15

    **Chapter 4: Animal Heroes**    22

    **Chapter 5: Animal Jobs**      28

  Ⓕ Chapter 1: Cat Tales

  Ⓖ Chapter 2: Amazing Dogs

  Ⓗ Chapter 3: In the Water

  Ⓘ Chapter 4: Animal Heroes

3. You see a word in dark type as you read. Where can you look to learn the meaning of the word?

  Ⓐ title page

  Ⓑ table of contents

  Ⓒ glossary

  Ⓓ index

4. What information would you find on the title page?

  Ⓕ the name of the author

  Ⓖ the title of the chapters

  Ⓗ the number of pages in the book

  Ⓘ the definitions of unknown words

TOTAL SCORE: _____ /4

Focus Skill: Locate Information      44

© Harcourt • Grade 3

---

Name _____

## Robust Vocabulary

▲ **Choose the word that best completes each sentence.**

**1.** Alexander Bell's well-known _____ is the telephone.

Ⓐ talented

Ⓑ invention

Ⓒ culture

Ⓓ anticipation

**2.** We didn't let the dark clouds _____ our picnic.

Ⓕ hinder

Ⓖ apply

Ⓗ dismiss

Ⓘ conquer

**3.** I was _____ when I didn't hit a home run.

Ⓐ pleasant

Ⓑ loyal

Ⓒ talented

Ⓓ disappointed

**4.** Tamika will _____ the life of astronaut John Glenn.

Ⓕ research

Ⓖ attain

Ⓗ hinder

Ⓘ apply

**5.** The _____ artist painted a lifelike picture.

Ⓐ certain

Ⓑ loyal

Ⓒ talented

Ⓓ confidence

**Robust Vocabulary**

47

---

Name _____

**2.** According to the dictionary, how many syllables are in the word *robot?*

Ⓕ one

Ⓖ two

Ⓗ three

Ⓘ four

**3.** How many entries are shown?

Ⓐ two

Ⓑ three

Ⓒ four

Ⓓ five

**4.** Which definition of *roar* is used in the sentence below?

**The crowd *roars* when the star player scores a point.**

Ⓕ *v.* To make a loud, deep growling noise

Ⓖ *v.* To laugh or cheer loudly or excitedly

Ⓗ *n.* The loud, deep cry of a wild animal

Ⓘ *n.* A loud noise made by something burning

**Use a Dictionary**

46

TOTAL SCORE: _____ /4

---

# Grammar: Compound Subjects and Predicates

▲ **Choose the best answer for each question.**

1. Which sentence has a compound subject?
   - (A) The puppy and the kitten became friends.
   - (B) The puppy learned a new trick.
   - (C) The kitten played with string.
   - (D) The puppy is napping next to the kitten.

2. Which sentence has a compound predicate?
   - (F) We drew a plan for the clubhouse.
   - (G) We bought wood from the store.
   - (H) We built and painted a clubhouse.
   - (I) Kim and I played in the clubhouse.

3. What is the correct way to join these two sentences?

   **The goat bit my shirt. The goat tugged on my shoelace.**

   - (A) The goat bit my shirt and the goat tugged on my shoelace.
   - (B) The goat bit my shirt and tugged on my shoelace.
   - (C) The goat bit my shirt tugged on my shoelace.
   - (D) The goat tugged my shirt and shoelace.

4. What is the correct way to join these two sentences?

   **Rosa went on vacation. Miriam went on vacation.**

   - (F) Rosa went on vacation and Miriam went on vacation.
   - (G) Rosa went on vacation and Miriam.
   - (H) Rosa went on vacation then Miriam went.
   - (J) Rosa and Miriam went on vacation.

**Grammar: Compound Subjects
and Predicates**
© Harcourt • Grade 3

`49`

TOTAL SCORE: _____ /4

---

6. She will _____ for the job at the office.
   - (F) hinder
   - (G) apply
   - (H) dismiss
   - (I) conquer

7. His _____ showed on his face as he started the race.
   - (A) invention
   - (B) confidence
   - (C) ambitious
   - (D) disappointed

8. He was determined to _____ his goal of early graduation.
   - (F) apply
   - (G) persevere
   - (H) attain
   - (I) imitated

9. Maria was _____ and decided to start a paper route.
   - (A) feature
   - (B) tutor
   - (C) confidence
   - (D) ambitious

10. Don't give up! You must _____ .
    - (F) persevere
    - (G) research
    - (H) apply
    - (I) hinder

**Robust Vocabulary**
© Harcourt • Grade 3

`48`

TOTAL SCORE: _____ /10

Name _____

## Selection Comprehension

▲ Choose the best answer for each question.

**1.** How are all the reporters the SAME?

　Ⓐ All talk about rain.

　Ⓑ All feed Freddy the Frog.

　Ⓒ All tell the news.

　Ⓓ All know how to play soccer.

**2.** What is unusual about today's lunch?

　Ⓕ New cooks will make the food.

　Ⓖ Children get two new choices.

　Ⓗ Children get to eat early.

　Ⓘ The food will cost less.

**3.** Where does most of the play take place?

　Ⓐ a playground

　Ⓑ a science classroom

　Ⓒ a television studio

　Ⓓ Mr. Moreno's office

**4.** The Science Reporter gets an award for

　Ⓕ taking Freddy home.

　Ⓖ learning more about a subject.

　Ⓗ telling people about frogs.

　Ⓘ being the best reporter on Kids News.

Selection Comprehension
"The School News"
© Harcourt • Grade 3

51

---

Name _____

## Oral Reading Fluency

| | |
|---|---:|
| Amanda was spending the night at her friend's house. | 9 |
| Amanda and Kayla had been friends since first grade. It | 19 |
| was quiet and dark in the living room, where the girls were | 31 |
| settled in their sleeping bags. | 36 |
| Suddenly, Amanda heard a noise. Her eyes jerked open. | 45 |
| "Kayla?" she called, but Kayla was asleep. | 52 |
| Amanda listened carefully, but the noise was gone. Just | 61 |
| as her eyes grew heavy, she heard the sound again. "What | 72 |
| is that?" she asked herself. "Is it a garbage truck? No, the | 84 |
| garbage truck wouldn't come at night. Is it an airplane? No, | 95 |
| that noise was louder than an airplane." | 102 |
| Amanda thought of waking Kayla, but the noise wasn't | 111 |
| scary. It was just loud. She clicked on the flashlight she and | 123 |
| Kayla had used earlier for reading. Slowly, she crawled out | 133 |
| of her sleeping bag. | 137 |
| As she walked toward the kitchen, the noise grew louder. | 147 |
| Amanda shone the beam around the kitchen. The noise was | 157 |
| very loud in here! Suddenly, she froze in her tracks! Then she | 169 |
| started laughing. Kayla's dog, Ruffy, was snoring! Amanda | 177- |
| laughed again and went back to the living room. | 186 |

_____ /WCPM

Oral Reading Fluency
© Harcourt • Grade 3

50

---

Name _____

**5.** Mr. Moreno reminds students to

   Ⓐ take books to the library.

   Ⓑ thank the visiting author.

   Ⓒ come to the office.

   Ⓓ read, read, read.

**6.** Which is the Science Reporter MOST LIKELY to talk about tomorrow?

   Ⓕ what the weather is like

   Ⓖ a book by the guest author

   Ⓗ the rules for playing soccer

   Ⓘ a new fish in the aquarium

**7.** How do the students MOST LIKELY feel about today's Sports Reporter's news?

   Ⓐ excited

   Ⓑ puzzled

   Ⓒ sorry

   Ⓓ upset

**8.** What must students do to sign up for the soccer team?

   Ⓕ read ten books

   Ⓖ see Coach Keller

   Ⓗ write a science report

   Ⓘ talk to Mr. Moreno

Selection Comprehension
"The School News"
© Harcourt • Grade 3

52

---

Name _____

READ
THINK
EXPLAIN

**Written Response** (worth two points)

**9.** Suppose you could be on Kids News. Would you like to be an anchor or one of the reporters? Explain why you would want that job. Use details from "The School News" to help you answer.

**Sample two-point response: I would like to be a science reporter. I like learning about science.**

_____

_____

_____

_____

Selection Comprehension
"The School News"
© Harcourt • Grade 3

53

TOTAL SCORE: _____ /8 + _____ /2

## Robust Vocabulary

▲ **Choose the word that best completes each sentence.**

1. I know you're nervous, but you will _____ the airplane ride.

Ⓐ camouflage
Ⓑ hinder
Ⓒ survive
Ⓓ dismiss

2. The boy ties his own shoes because he wants to be _____.

Ⓕ independent
Ⓖ popular
Ⓗ disappointed
Ⓘ certain

3. I _____ my excitement when I made the team.

Ⓐ squirmed
Ⓑ disappointed
Ⓒ donated
Ⓓ concealed

4. The hunter wore _____ in the woods.

Ⓕ patchwork
Ⓖ camouflage
Ⓗ uniforms
Ⓘ resources

5. We _____ food to the people who lost their homes.

Ⓐ modeled
Ⓑ donated
Ⓒ talented
Ⓓ concealed

---

6. The _____ watched the news event as it happened.

Ⓕ uniforms
Ⓖ patchwork
Ⓗ viewers
Ⓘ resources

7. Because it's fun, bicycling is a _____ form of exercise.

Ⓐ camouflage
Ⓑ donated
Ⓒ concealed
Ⓓ popular

8. The exhibit will _____ artwork from young artists.

Ⓕ feature
Ⓖ image
Ⓗ survive
Ⓘ persevere

9. News reports are one type of _____.

Ⓐ popular
Ⓑ camouflage
Ⓒ viewers
Ⓓ media

10. What _____ do you see on the screen?

Ⓕ camouflage
Ⓖ package
Ⓗ image
Ⓘ media

TOTAL SCORE: _____ /10

## Selection Comprehension

▲ Choose the best answer for each question.

1. How can readers tell "The Babe and I" is historical fiction?

   (A) It has a real person and has events that could have happened.

   (B) It has directions telling where characters are on a stage.

   (C) It tells about a mystery that characters try to solve.

   (D) It explains how people and places came to be.

2. What secret is Dad keeping in the story?

   (F) He does not have a real job.

   (G) He is saving for a new bicycle.

   (H) He has started selling newspapers.

   (I) He has tickets to watch Babe Ruth play.

3. Why is the narrator sorry after he spends his birthday dime?

   (A) He needs the money to buy a newspaper.

   (B) He sees something else that he wants to buy.

   (C) He does not like the taste of the apples he buys.

   (D) He knows how hard his dad worked for the money.

4. How does Babe Ruth help the narrator sell papers?

   (F) by giving the narrator a job

   (G) by having lots of money to spend

   (H) by being a famous baseball player

   (I) by telling others to buy from the narrator

5. How does Dad MOST LIKELY feel when the narrator tells him that he was once on Webster Avenue?

   (A) ashamed

   (B) curious

   (C) lucky

   (D) brave

6. What is the MAIN reason Jacob and the narrator sell more papers than other people?

   (F) They stand near a busy apartment building.

   (G) They know people are interested in baseball.

   (H) They call out the headlines in a loud voice.

   (I) They are strong and can carry many papers.

7. Why doesn't the narrator recognize Babe Ruth when Babe gives him a five-dollar bill?

   (A) Babe does not have on his baseball clothes.

   (B) Babe is too tall for the narrator to see his face.

   (C) Babe looks older than his pictures in the paper.

   (D) Babe uses another name when he talks to the narrator.

8. How are the narrator and his dad ALIKE?

   (F) They both play baseball.

   (G) They are both "newsies."

   (H) They both earn money.

   (I) They both sell apples.

Name _____

## Phonics/Spelling: Compound Words

▲ Choose the best answer for each question.

1. How should you divide the word <u>starfish</u> into two words?
   - (A) starf-ish
   - (B) sta-rfish
   - (C) star-fish
   - (D) starfi-sh

2. How should you divide the word <u>afternoon</u> into two words?
   - (F) after-noon
   - (G) aft-ernoon
   - (H) afte-rnoon
   - (I) aftern-oon

3. How should you divide the word <u>popcorn</u> into two words?
   - (A) po-pcorn
   - (B) pop-corn
   - (C) popc-orn
   - (D) p-opcorn

4. How should you divide the word <u>sunshine</u> into two words?
   - (F) suns-hine
   - (G) su-nshine
   - (H) sunsh-ine
   - (I) sun-shine

Phonics/Spelling: Compound Words

59

© Harcourt • Grade 3

TOTAL SCORE: _____ /4

---

Name _____

READ
THINK
EXPLAIN

## Written Response (worth two points)

9. **COMPARING TEXTS** At the time this story took place, why were people so interested in reading about Babe Ruth? Use information and details from "The Babe and I" AND the time line "America's National Pastime" to support your answer.

**Sample two-point response:** In 1927, Babe had hit 60

home runs in one season. No one broke his record for

34 years. When this story took place, he was the world's

greatest baseball player. His team was the best in the

world.

_____

Selection Comprehension
"The Babe and I"
© Harcourt • Grade 3

58

TOTAL SCORE: _____ /8 + _____ /2

## Focus Skill: Fact and Opinion

▲ Read the passage. Then choose the best answer for each question.

### The Best Season

Winter is the best season of the year! There is so much to do, especially if you live where it snows. Some places, like Marquette, Michigan, get more than 130 inches of snow each year. Think of all the things you can do with that much snow! You can go skiing or snowshoeing. You can build a snowman or ride a snowmobile. I think the best thing to do is to go sledding. Afterward, you can have hot chocolate!

Everyone should go to an ice hotel. There is one in Canada. Each year workers build a hotel entirely out of ice and snow! Even the furniture, artwork, and light fixtures are made of ice! The worst part is that it all goes away in early April. In April, the temperature rises and the ice melts. I hope I can stay in an ice hotel this winter!

1. Which of the following is an opinion from the first paragraph?

Ⓐ I think the best thing to do is to go sledding.
Ⓑ You can build a snowman or ride a snowmobile.
Ⓒ Afterward, you can have hot chocolate!
Ⓓ You can go skiing or snowshoeing.

---

2. How can you tell whether a sentence is a fact?

Ⓕ It tells what the author thinks.
Ⓖ It tells what the author believes is true.
Ⓗ It can be seen or proved.
Ⓘ It cannot be proved to be true or false.

3. Which is a statement of fact from the selection?

Ⓐ Winter is the best season of the year!
Ⓑ Some places, like Marquette, Michigan, get more than 130 inches of snow each year.
Ⓒ I think the best thing to do is to go sledding.
Ⓓ Everyone should go to an ice hotel.

4. Which is an opinion from the selection?

Ⓕ There is an ice hotel in Canada.
Ⓖ Each year, workers build a hotel entirely of ice and snow!
Ⓗ The worst part is that it all goes away in early April.
Ⓘ In April, the temperature rises and the ice melts.

TOTAL SCORE: _____ /4

## Synonyms and Antonyms

▲ **Choose the best answer for each question.**

**1.** Read this sentence.

**The bike is easy to repair.**

What is a synonym of the word *repair?*

Ⓐ ride
**Ⓑ fix**
Ⓒ see
Ⓓ pedal

**2.** Read this sentence.

**The dog can fetch the paper.**

What is a synonym of the word *fetch?*

Ⓕ tear
Ⓖ see
**Ⓗ bring**
Ⓘ chew

**3.** Read this sentence.

**That dog is huge!**

What is an antonym of the word *huge?*

Ⓐ cute
Ⓑ large
**Ⓒ tiny**
Ⓓ trained

**4.** Read this sentence.

**My brother and I sometimes argue.**

What is an antonym of the word *argue?*

Ⓕ talk
**Ⓖ agree**
Ⓗ fight
Ⓘ play

**5.** Read this sentence.

**Why are you weeping?**

What is an antonym of the word *weeping?*

Ⓐ jogging
Ⓑ eating
Ⓒ sleeping
**Ⓓ laughing**

TOTAL SCORE: _____ /5

Name _____

## Robust Vocabulary

▲ **Choose the word that best completes each sentence.**

1. If you tell that story, you will _____ me.
   (A) embarrass
   (B) survive
   (C) apply
   (D) tutor

2. The doctor made her keep her foot _____ until it healed.
   (F) independent
   (G) dazed
   (H) elevated
   (I) talented

3. The team shirt was _____ by the end of the season.
   (A) pleasant
   (B) shabby
   (C) disappointed
   (D) certain

4. I was _____ by the bright lights.
   (F) dazed
   (G) elevated
   (H) squirmed
   (I) modeled

5. A famous soccer player is in the team's _____.
   (A) resources
   (B) invention
   (C) midst
   (D) culture

Name _____

6. What happens if the bridge _____?
   (F) collapses
   (G) concealed
   (H) resources
   (I) independent

7. Sometimes you can _____ a passage to locate information.
   (A) span
   (B) skim
   (C) embarrass
   (D) survive

8. The man made a large _____ to the animal shelter.
   (F) contribution
   (G) donated
   (H) midst
   (I) initiative

9. She took the _____ to start a food drive.
   (A) image
   (B) shabby
   (C) initiative
   (D) span

10. The workers built the bridge to _____ the river.
    (F) skim
    (G) survive
    (H) embarrass
    (I) span

Robust Vocabulary

© Harcourt • Grade 3

64

Robust Vocabulary

© Harcourt • Grade 3

65

TOTAL SCORE: _____ /10

## Grammar: Simple and Compound Sentences

▲ **Choose the best answer for each question.**

**1.** Read this sentence.

I wanted to play baseball, but we played soccer.

Is this a compound sentence? Why?

Ⓐ No. It has only one period.

Ⓑ No. It has only one subject and one predicate.

Ⓒ Yes. The parts are joined by a comma and a conjunction.

Ⓓ Yes. It contains a compound subject.

**2.** Which of the following is a compound sentence?

Ⓕ I like to draw, and my sister likes to sing.

Ⓖ My sister is eight years old.

Ⓗ Yesterday after school, I drew a picture.

Ⓘ Jayna likes to sing and dance.

**3.** What is the correct way to join these two sentences?

I wanted to hear the lion roar. He was sleeping.

Ⓐ I wanted to hear the lion roar and he was sleeping.

Ⓑ I wanted to hear the lion roar, but he was sleeping.

Ⓒ The lion was sleeping but I wanted to hear him roar.

Ⓓ The lion, I wanted to hear him roar but he was sleeping.

**4.** What is the correct way to join these two sentences?

Matt went to the park. He met a new friend.

Ⓕ At the new park, Matt met a friend when he went.

Ⓖ He met a new friend, Matt did, at the park.

Ⓗ Matt went to the park and he met a new friend.

Ⓘ Matt went to the park, and he met a new friend.

Grammar: Simple and Compound
Sentences
© Harcourt • Grade 3

66

TOTAL SCORE: _____ /4

---

## Oral Reading Fluency

Have nurses ever held your wrist and told you to be      11
quiet? If so, do you know what they were doing and why      23
it was important?      26

You probably know that your heart pumps blood. Did      35
you know that blood travels in tubes, called arteries, from      45
your heart to all parts of your body? Some of these tiny      57
tubes are in your wrist.      62

Each time your heart beats, it squeezes blood into your      72
arteries. When this happens, the tubes bulge. The bulging      81
is called your pulse. When nurses hold your wrist, they feel      92
and count the bulges to find out how fast your heart is      104
beating.      105

You can feel your pulse in other places, too. Put your      116
index and middle fingers together, and then press them      125
gently on your neck, just below your chin. Count the      135
number of bulges, or beats, you feel in one minute. This      146
count tells you your heart rate, or the number of times      157
your heart beats in one minute. Your heart rate is lower      168
when you are resting. Worrying or exercising can increase      177
your heart rate.      180

Oral Reading Fluency
© Harcourt • Grade 3

67

_____ /WCPM

Name _____

## Selection Comprehension

▲ Choose the best answer for each question.

1. How can readers tell this passage is nonfiction?
   - (A) It has events that could never happen.
   - (B) It is set in the past and tells about history.
   - (C) It tells why one person became important.
   - (D) It tells about a real dog and a real police officer.

2. What does this passage MAINLY tell?
   - (F) how Aero helps his partner
   - (G) what Aero likes to do for fun
   - (H) where Aero began his training
   - (I) why Aero goes to visit schools

3. What is Aero's main job?
   - (A) to walk up steep stairs
   - (B) to protect Officer Mike
   - (C) to walk over open grates
   - (D) to go through hard spots

4. How is Aero DIFFERENT from most other dogs?
   - (F) He likes to have his tummy scratched.
   - (G) He can understand another language.
   - (H) He chases balls and explores.
   - (I) He often sleeps on the floor.

Selection Comprehension
"Aero and Officer Mike"
© Harcourt • Grade 3

---

Name _____

5. What MOST helps Aero find missing people?
   - (A) his strong jaws
   - (B) his sharp teeth
   - (C) his sense of smell
   - (D) his powerful legs

6. How are Officer Mike and Aero ALIKE?
   - (F) Both explain rules about petting dogs.
   - (G) Both make a report about their day.
   - (H) Both can run forty miles an hour.
   - (I) Both wear a police badge.

7. When chasing someone, what is Aero MOST LIKELY to do if he comes to a fence that is six feet high?
   - (A) jump over it
   - (B) stop and wait
   - (C) return to the car
   - (D) bark and call for help

8. Which sentence is an OPINION in the passage?
   - (F) Officer Mike and Aero are partners.
   - (G) They both love being police officers.
   - (H) Officer Mike sits in the driver's seat.
   - (I) Aero lies down by Officer Mike's chair.

Selection Comprehension
"Aero and Officer Mike"
© Harcourt • Grade 3

---

Name _____

## Phonics/Spelling: Digraphs /ch/ch, tch; /sh/sh, ch; /(h)w/wh

▲ Read each model word. Then fill in the circle next to the word that has the same sound as the underlined part of the model word and completes each sentence.

**1. hatch**

We will _____ for our school's soccer team.

- Ⓐ cheer
- Ⓑ count
- Ⓒ call
- Ⓓ shout

**2. wheat**

That blue _____ is huge!

- Ⓕ whole
- Ⓖ hawk
- Ⓗ whale
- Ⓘ wrap

**3. dash**

I found a beautiful _____ on the beach.

- Ⓐ watch
- Ⓑ shell
- Ⓒ sand
- Ⓓ wave

**4. chef**

The dog is sleeping in the _____ of that tree.

- Ⓕ center
- Ⓖ straw
- Ⓗ chair
- Ⓘ shade

TOTAL SCORE: _____ /4

---

Name _____

READ
THINK
EXPLAIN

## Written Response (worth two points)

9. Explain why dogs make good helpers for police officers. Use details and information from "Aero and Officer Mike" to support your answer.

**Sample two-point response: Dogs have a good sense of**

**smell, so they can find lost people. They can run fast,**

**and they obey orders.**

TOTAL SCORE: _____ /8 + _____ /2

**Focus Skill: Fact and Opinion**

▲ Read the passage. Then choose the best answer for each question.

## Popular Pets

Many people in the United States own pets. Some households have one pet, and others have several. What kinds of pets do Americans have? Let's take a look!

Dogs and cats are the most popular pets. About 40 million homes have one or more dogs as pets. Almost 35 million homes have one or more cats as pets. Dogs make better pets because they are friendlier. However, cats are the best pets for people who do not have a yard.

Fish are also popular pets. You can find fish in about 12 million homes. Fish are fun to watch, but they are too much trouble. You must keep their water clean and warm.

More than 5 million homes own a small animal, such as a rabbit or hamster. These animals do not make good pets. They often smell and do not live as long as a cat or dog. Everyone should have a pet!

1. What question can you ask yourself to decide whether a statement is an opinion?
   (A) Is this sentence interesting?
   (B) Is this what someone thinks or feels but cannot prove?
   (C) Is this an important part of the selection I'm reading?
   (D) Do I agree with this statement?

2. Which is true about a statement of fact?
   (F) It describes the author's beliefs.
   (G) It is contained in an opinion.
   (H) It can be seen or proved.
   (I) It is less interesting than someone's opinion.

3. Which is a statement of fact?
   (A) About 40 million homes have one or more dogs as pets.
   (B) Dogs make better pets because they are friendlier.
   (C) Fish are fun to watch, but they are too much trouble.
   (D) Everyone should have a pet!

4. Which is the author's opinion?
   (F) Some households have one pet, and others have several.
   (G) Dogs and cats are the most popular pets.
   (H) Cats are the best pets for people who do not have a yard.
   (I) You can find fish in about 12 million homes.

TOTAL SCORE: _____ /4

# Synonyms and Antonyms

▲ Choose the best answer for each question.

**1.** Read this sentence.

It is noisy in the cafeteria.

What is a synonym of the word *noisy?*

Ⓐ busy
Ⓑ loud
Ⓒ crowded
Ⓓ calm

**2.** Read this sentence.

Do not leave your bicycle on the lawn.

What is a synonym of the word *lawn?*

Ⓕ dock
Ⓖ driveway
Ⓗ street
Ⓘ yard

**3.** Read this sentence.

She won an award for the best poem.

What is a synonym of the word *award?*

Ⓐ prize
Ⓑ frame
Ⓒ paper
Ⓓ nickel

Synonyms and Antonyms

© Harcourt • Grade 3

**74**

---

**4.** Read this sentence.

To solve the problem, you must add the numbers.

What is an antonym of the word *add?*

Ⓕ write
Ⓖ total
Ⓗ subtract
Ⓘ name

**5.** Read this sentence.

Do not forget your homework!

What is an antonym of the word *forget?*

Ⓐ remember
Ⓑ leave
Ⓒ lose
Ⓓ finish

Synonyms and Antonyms

© Harcourt • Grade 3

**75**

TOTAL SCORE: _____/5

Name _____

# Robust Vocabulary

▲ Choose the word that best completes each sentence.

1. I smelled the strong _____ of onions cooking.
   - Ⓐ patrol
   - Ⓑ competent
   - Ⓒ scent
   - Ⓓ babble

2. We couldn't understand the child's _____.
   - Ⓕ babble
   - Ⓖ scent
   - Ⓗ wanders
   - Ⓘ whined

3. Our dog _____ away if he gets out of the fence.
   - Ⓐ collapses
   - Ⓑ whined
   - Ⓒ wanders
   - Ⓓ suspicious

4. She became _____ when she saw her brother carrying a cake.
   - Ⓕ popular
   - Ⓖ suspicious
   - Ⓗ elevated
   - Ⓘ competent

5. The secretary is _____ at preparing documents.
   - Ⓐ concealed
   - Ⓑ suspicious
   - Ⓒ demonstrate
   - Ⓓ competent

Robust Vocabulary

© Harcourt • Grade 3

76

---

Name _____

6. My younger brother _____ about eating his dinner.
   - Ⓕ wandered
   - Ⓖ elevated
   - Ⓗ whined
   - Ⓘ donated

7. Our dog thinks his job is to _____ his yard.
   - Ⓐ patrol
   - Ⓑ babble
   - Ⓒ obey
   - Ⓓ accompany

8. When you take a test, you can _____ your knowledge.
   - Ⓕ obey
   - Ⓖ demonstrate
   - Ⓗ accompany
   - Ⓘ babble

9. You should always _____ your parents.
   - Ⓐ patrol
   - Ⓑ suspicious
   - Ⓒ demonstrate
   - Ⓓ obey

10. Will you _____ me to the concert?
   - Ⓕ competent
   - Ⓖ accompany
   - Ⓗ obey
   - Ⓘ patrol

Robust Vocabulary

© Harcourt • Grade 3

77

TOTAL SCORE: _____ /10

## Grammar: Common and Proper Nouns

▲ **Read each sentence. Choose the word that is a proper noun that should begin with a capital letter.**

1. The biggest city in the world is tokyo.
   - Ⓐ biggest
   - Ⓑ city
   - Ⓒ world
   - Ⓓ tokyo

2. Is saturn the planet that has rings made of ice?
   - Ⓕ saturn
   - Ⓖ planet
   - Ⓗ rings
   - Ⓘ ice

3. My family celebrates thanksgiving with a large meal.
   - Ⓐ family
   - Ⓑ celebrates
   - Ⓒ thanksgiving
   - Ⓓ meal

4. Aisha's grandparents live in new york city.
   - Ⓕ grandparents
   - Ⓖ live
   - Ⓗ in
   - Ⓘ new york city

TOTAL SCORE: _____ /4

---

## Oral Reading Fluency

| | |
|---|---|
| Last weekend we had a picnic in our neighborhood to | 10 |
| celebrate the end of summer. I saw one of our neighbors, a little | 23 |
| girl named Margaret. Margaret was going to start kindergarten | 33 |
| in a few days. I asked her whether she was excited about | 44 |
| school. She told me that she was, but she looked ready to cry. | 55 |
| I knew that she had gone to half-day preschool, so I said, | 67 |
| "You'll stay at school all day this year! Isn't that exciting?" | 78 |
| She nodded and walked away. I followed her over to her | 89 |
| mother, and I heard Margaret ask how long she'd stay in | 100 |
| kindergarten. Her mother said that she'd stay all day. | 109 |
| "So, will I miss dinner at home and will I get home when it's | 123 |
| dark outside?" Margaret asked with a brave face. | 131 |
| "Oh, no!" her mother responded. "You won't stay all day, | 141 |
| The bus will bring you home at 3 o'clock." | 150 |
| On the first day of school I saw Margaret on the bus. | 162 |
| "I didn't learn everything today," she said. "So they're | 171 |
| making me come back tomorrow." | 176 |
| Boy, does she have a lot to learn! | 184 |

_____ /WCPM

## Selection Comprehension

▲ Choose the best answer for each question.

1. Why did the author write this passage?

  Ⓐ to teach how to take care of animals

  Ⓑ to persuade people to protect animals

  Ⓒ to describe one special kind of animal

  Ⓓ to tell ways that animals send messages

2. How can readers tell that "How Animals Talk" is nonfiction?

  Ⓕ It tells events in time order.

  Ⓖ It gives true facts about a subject.

  Ⓗ It tells why a person is important.

  Ⓘ It has characters that must solve a problem.

3. What is MOST LIKELY happening when two bull elks crash their horns together?

  Ⓐ They are showing their power.

  Ⓑ They are greeting each other.

  Ⓒ They are telling others where they are.

  Ⓓ They are warning each other of danger.

4. How does the passage say that male deer tell other deer to stay away?

  Ⓕ They howl loudly.

  Ⓖ They raise their backs.

  Ⓗ They rub a smell on trees.

  Ⓘ They make a snorting sound.

5. Sailors used to compare the beluga whale to a canary because the canary

  Ⓐ sings a sweet song.

  Ⓑ flies near the sea.

  Ⓒ has a bright color.

  Ⓓ lives a long time.

6. The author uses the pictures of the baby robins with their mouths open to show

  Ⓕ how robins ask to be fed.

  Ⓖ how robins catch their food.

  Ⓗ what kind of food robins eat.

  Ⓘ how robins hide from enemies.

7. If "How Animals Talk" needed a new title, which would be BEST?

  Ⓐ "How to Choose a Pet"

  Ⓑ "What Did That Bird Say?"

  Ⓒ "Let's Visit an Animal Farm"

  Ⓓ "Which Animals Run the Fastest?"

8. Which event is MOST LIKELY to cause a male white-tailed deer to turn up its tail?

  Ⓕ getting lost

  Ⓖ feeling hungry

  Ⓗ seeing an enemy

  Ⓘ meeting a friend

## Phonics/Spelling: Diphthongs

▲ Read each model word. Then fill in the circle next to the word that has the same sound as the underlined part of the model word and completes each sentence.

**1. toy**

I found a _____ on the sidewalk and put it in my pocket.

Ⓐ cloth

Ⓑ cookie

Ⓒ coat

● coin

**2. owl**

The _____ noise woke the baby.

Ⓕ load

● loud

Ⓗ low

Ⓘ large

**3. join**

Did you hear about the _____ who saved his sister's life?

Ⓐ bought

Ⓑ brother

● boy

Ⓓ blow

**4. proud**

The _____ leaves on the trail crunched under our feet.

● brown

Ⓖ bought

Ⓗ bush

Ⓘ bold

---

READ
THINK
EXPLAIN

### Written Response (worth two points)

9. Explain why it is important for animals to send messages to each other. Use details and information from "How Animals Talk" to support your answer.

Sample two-point response: Animals need to be able to

warn each other when they are in danger. They also need

to be able to scare away their enemies, to tell each other

where they are, and to show who is the strongest.

## Focus Skill: Main Idea and Details

▲ Read the passages. Then choose the best answer for each question.

### Presidents' Pets

The President and First Lady are not the only ones who live in the White House. Many Presidents bring pets into the White House. There have been some pretty unusual First Pets!

Dogs are popular pets in our country, so it is no surprise that many have lived in the White House. George W. Bush brought Spot the dog to live in the White House. When Bill Clinton was President, he had a Labrador named Buddy. He also had a cat named Socks.

Calvin Coolidge was President from 1923 to 1929. He had 12 dogs and two cats. He also had a bear, two raccoons, a bobcat, and a hippo. Most of the odd pets were gifts from other governments or groups.

1. What is the main idea of the passage?
   Ⓐ The President and First Lady live in the White House.
   Ⓑ Pets often live in the White House.
   Ⓒ Dogs are popular pets in the United States.
   Ⓓ Calvin Coolidge had many pets when he was President.

2. Which detail supports this main idea?
   **Some presidents have unusual pets.**
   Ⓕ Many Presidents bring pets into the White House.
   Ⓖ He also had a cat named Socks.
   Ⓗ Calvin Coolidge was President from 1923 to 1929.
   Ⓘ Calvin Coolidge also had a bear, two raccoons, a bobcat, and a hippo.

Focus Skill: Main Idea and Details          84

© Harcourt • Grade 3

---

### Animal Homes

Animals have different kinds of homes. Pets live with people, but many animals must find or build their own shelters. Different animals have different ways of making their homes.

Some animals dig into the ground. Earthworms dig tunnels and live in the soil. Badgers use their strong front paws to dig into the ground. Polar bears dig into packed snow to make a warm den.

Some animals build their homes above the ground. Beavers use mud and branches to build lodges. Termites build towering nests. Some can be 10 feet tall!

3. What is the main idea of the selection?
   Ⓐ Some animals dig their homes into the ground.
   Ⓑ Animals build different kinds of homes.
   Ⓒ Pets live with people in their homes.
   Ⓓ Beavers build their homes with mud and branches.

4. Which main idea does this detail support?
   **Termites build towering nests.**
   Ⓕ Some animals build their homes above the ground.
   Ⓖ Pets live with people.
   Ⓗ Some animals dig into the ground.
   Ⓘ Polar bears dig into packed snow to make a warm den.

Focus Skill: Main Idea and Details          85

© Harcourt • Grade 3

TOTAL SCORE: _____ /4

Name _____

## Use Reference Sources

▲ Use the encyclopedias below to answer each question.

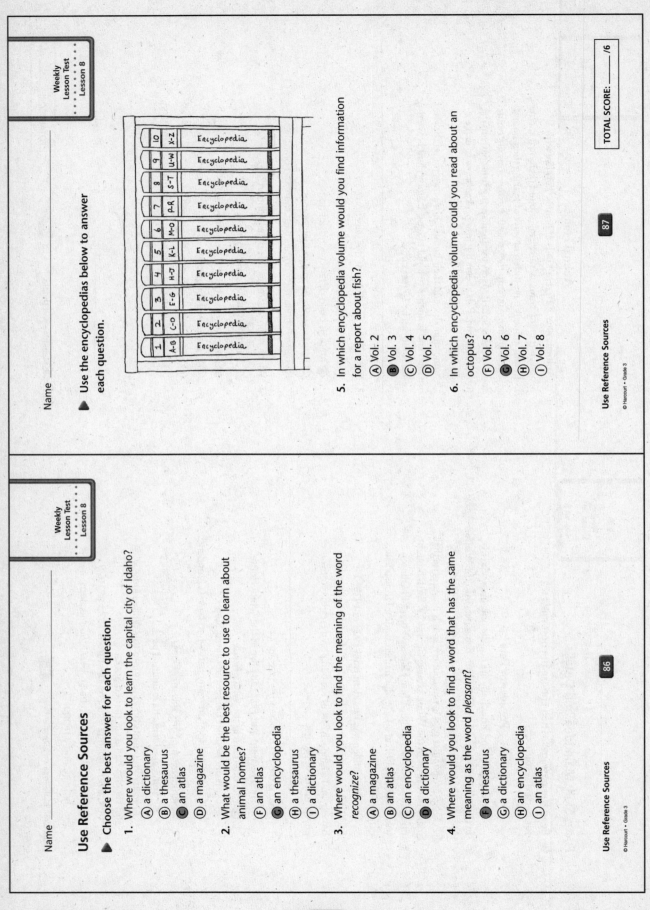

5. In which encyclopedia volume would you find information for a report about fish?

  Ⓐ Vol. 2
  Ⓑ Vol. 3
  Ⓒ Vol. 4
  Ⓓ Vol. 5

6. In which encyclopedia volume could you read about an octopus?

  Ⓕ Vol. 5
  Ⓖ Vol. 6
  Ⓗ Vol. 7
  Ⓘ Vol. 8

Use Reference Sources    87

TOTAL SCORE: _____ /6

© Harcourt • Grade 3

---

Name _____

## Use Reference Sources

▲ Choose the best answer for each question.

1. Where would you look to learn the capital city of Idaho?

  Ⓐ a dictionary
  Ⓑ a thesaurus
  Ⓒ an atlas
  Ⓓ a magazine

2. What would be the best resource to use to learn about animal homes?

  Ⓕ an atlas
  Ⓖ an encyclopedia
  Ⓗ a thesaurus
  Ⓘ a dictionary

3. Where would you look to find the meaning of the word *recognize*?

  Ⓐ a magazine
  Ⓑ an atlas
  Ⓒ an encyclopedia
  Ⓓ a dictionary

4. Where would you look to find a word that has the same meaning as the word *pleasant*?

  Ⓕ a thesaurus
  Ⓖ a dictionary
  Ⓗ an encyclopedia
  Ⓘ an atlas

Use Reference Sources    86

© Harcourt • Grade 3

Name _____

# Robust Vocabulary

▲ Choose the word that best completes each sentence.

1. The mother chimp _____ her baby.
   - **(A) grooms**
   - (B) communicates
   - (C) wanders
   - (D) demonstrates

2. You must _____ the game spinner when it is your turn.
   - (F) communicate
   - (G) signal
   - (H) alert
   - **(I) flick**

3. What _____ is the coach giving the player?
   - (A) conflict
   - (B) flick
   - **(C) signal**
   - (D) chatter

4. The _____ lion caught its prey.
   - (F) dazed
   - **(G) ferocious**
   - (H) shabby
   - (I) suspicious

5. The _____ gorilla rules his group.
   - (A) signal
   - (B) chatter
   - (C) alert
   - **(D) dominant**

Robust Vocabulary

88

© Harcourt • Grade 3

---

Name _____

6. We heard the _____ coming from the classroom.
   - (F) camouflage
   - (G) patrol
   - **(H) chatter**
   - (I) charging

7. Writing letters is my favorite way to _____.
   - **(A) communicate**
   - (B) flick
   - (C) chatter
   - (D) groom

8. I ended the _____ with my brother.
   - (F) scent
   - (G) charging
   - **(H) conflict**
   - (I) alert

9. The dog went _____ after the cat.
   - (A) disappointed
   - **(B) charging**
   - (C) dominant
   - (D) ferocious

10. The whistle will _____ the students that recess is over.
   - **(F) alert**
   - (G) communicate
   - (H) conflict
   - (I) groom

Robust Vocabulary

89

© Harcourt • Grade 3

TOTAL SCORE: _____ /10

---

## Grammar: Abbreviations

▲ Read each word. Write the letter of the
abbreviation that matches it.

1. **e** Street

2. **i** Mister

3. **f** Monday

4. **b** Texas

5. **a** Doctor

6. **j** October

7. **d** Avenue

8. **c** California

9. **g** Friday

10. **h** February

a. Dr.

b. TX

c. CA

d. Ave.

e. St.

f. Mon.

g. Fri.

h. Feb.

i. Mr.

j. Oct.

TOTAL SCORE: _____ /10

Grammar: Abbreviations

© Harcourt • Grade 3

90

## Oral Reading Fluency

A wolf is a member of the dog family. Unlike pet dogs, 12
wild wolves are not good companions for humans. They 21
are ferocious hunters. 24

Wolves live in groups called packs. Wolves in a pack 34
communicate with one another. One way they do this 43
is by howling. Many people think a wolf's howl is a 54
frightening sound. They often say wolves howl at the 63
moon. The truth is, wolves howl for different reasons. 72

A wolf might howl to tell the rest of the pack that they 85
should come together to start a hunt. Because wolves 94
hunt mostly at night, the moon happens to be out. A 105
wolf may howl to tell another animal to stay out of the 117
wolves' territory. If a wolf gets separated from the pack, it 128
may howl to tell the other pack members where it is. 139

Like our pet dogs, wolves also bark and growl. What 149
does it mean when a dog barks or growls? A wolf's bark 161
or growl might mean the same thing. A wolf uses these 172
sounds to say, "I'm angry!" 177

_____ /WCPM

Oral Reading Fluency

© Harcourt • Grade 3

91

## Selection Comprehension

▲ Choose the best answer for each question.

1. What is "Stone Soup" MOST LIKE?

   Ⓐ a play

   Ⓑ a tall tale

   Ⓒ a folktale

   Ⓓ a mystery

2. Why didn't anyone answer when the monks first knocked on the villagers' doors?

   Ⓕ They were not at home.

   Ⓖ They did not trust strangers.

   Ⓗ They did not hear anyone outside.

   Ⓘ They thought someone might ask for money.

3. What is the villagers' BIGGEST problem in the story?

   Ⓐ They are not friendly with each other.

   Ⓑ They do not have enough food to eat.

   Ⓒ They have to work too hard.

   Ⓓ Their village has flooded.

4. What is the main reason why the soup tastes delicious?

   Ⓕ The monks used special stones.

   Ⓖ Everyone added more to the pot.

   Ⓗ The scholar added extra spices.

   Ⓘ Carrots made the soup sweet.

---

5. What can readers tell about the three monks?

   Ⓐ They have probably made stone soup before.

   Ⓑ They have visited this village before.

   Ⓒ They have not traveled far.

   Ⓓ They are all the same age.

6. The monks help the villagers learn how to

   Ⓕ tell stories.

   Ⓖ sing songs.

   Ⓗ build a fire.

   Ⓘ share what they have.

7. What is MOST LIKELY to happen next?

   Ⓐ The monks will stay in the village to cook for everyone.

   Ⓑ The villagers will argue about what to put in the soup.

   Ⓒ The monks will make dumplings for the Emperor.

   Ⓓ The villagers will eat meals together more often.

8. What is the MOST important lesson the villagers learn in this story?

   Ⓕ Anything tastes good when you are hungry.

   Ⓖ Save for bad times while you have plenty.

   Ⓗ The more you give, the more you get.

   Ⓘ Slow cooking makes foods taste better.

## Phonics/Spelling: Consonant Blends

▲ Read each model word. Then fill in the circle next to the word that has the same sound as the underlined part of the model word and completes each sentence.

**1. scream**

The cat _____ me when it tried to get away from the dog.

- Ⓐ scrape
- Ⓑ struck
- Ⓒ scratched
- Ⓓ stretched

**2. spray**

First, _____ the peanut butter on the bread.

- Ⓕ spread
- Ⓖ scratch
- Ⓗ streak
- Ⓘ sprain

**3. stretch**

May I please have a _____ for my drink?

- Ⓐ screen
- Ⓑ straw
- Ⓒ strong
- Ⓓ spoon

**4. scrap**

We had to _____ the floor to get the dirt off of it.

- Ⓕ scrub
- Ⓖ spray
- Ⓗ screech
- Ⓘ string

Phonics/Spelling: Consonant Blends
str, scr, spr
© Harcourt • Grade 3

TOTAL SCORE: _____ /4

95

---

READ
THINK
EXPLAIN

## Written Response (worth two points)

**9.** Explain how the villagers changed during the story. Use details and information from "Stone Soup" to support your answer.

Sample two-point response: At first, the villagers kept

to themselves too much. They were suspicious of each

other. When they started helping to make the soup, each

person had something to give that made the soup better.

Working together and sharing make the villagers happy.

Selection Comprehension
"Stone Soup"
© Harcourt • Grade 3

TOTAL SCORE: _____ /8 + _____ /2

94

## April Fools' Day

April Fools' Day is a great day. I love to play tricks on people. Of course, I would never play a trick that was mean or hurtful. No, I like to play light-hearted tricks on my friends and family.

I have really long hair. One year, I woke up extra early and used hairpins to pin my hair under so that it looked as if it came up to my chin. My family and friends at school thought I'd cut my hair. A few years ago, we planted a vegetable garden in the backyard. With Mom's help, I stuck vegetables from the store in their place. Everyone thought the seeds grew amazingly fast! Last year, I put a spool of thread inside my dad's coat pocket and pulled a little section of it though the top. I pretended to find it that morning and began pulling it. I kept pulling and it kept coming out. Finally, Dad realized what I'd done. He laughed and laughed.

3. What is the main idea of the passage?
   A Vegetables grow faster in April.
   B The author's dad does not like April Fools'.
   C A good trick to play on people is to cut your hair.
   ● D The author likes to play jokes on April Fools' Day.

4. Which detail supports this main idea?

   **A good practical joke can make people happy.**
   ● F The author's dad laughed at the thread joke.
   G People thought the seeds grew really fast.
   H The author plays light-hearted tricks on people.
   I People thought the author really cut her hair.

Focus Skill: Main Idea and Details      97

TOTAL SCORE: _____ /4

© Harcourt • Grade 3

---

## Focus Skill: Main Idea and Details

▲ Read the passages. Then choose the best answer for each question.

### A New Sprinkler

Have you ever solved a problem? If so, you may have made an invention! Kids can be great inventors.

Larry was a child and an inventor. He noticed a problem. When he had to water the lawn, he wasted a lot of water moving the hose and sprinkler to different trees. To solve the problem, he got a round sprinkler, cut out a section, and sealed the ends. He made a sprinkler that fit around the base of a tree. He put holes in both the top and bottom of the sprinkler and tested his new invention.

It worked! Larry won an invention contest at school. He began making and selling them. Today, thousands of people have one of Larry's sprinklers.

1. What is the main idea of the passage?
   A Inventions solve problems.
   B Kids can be great inventors.
   ● C A child named Larry invented a sprinkler.
   D Wasting water when watering plants is not a problem.

2. Which detail supports this main idea?

   **Larry's water sprinkler was successful.**
   ● F Today, thousands of people have one of Larry's sprinklers.
   G Larry is a child inventor.
   H He noticed a problem.
   I If so, you may have made an invention!

Focus Skill: Main Idea and Details      96

© Harcourt • Grade 3

---

*Student Edition pp. 96–97*

79

© Harcourt • Grade 3

## Use Reference Sources

▲ Choose the best answer for each question.

1. You are writing a report. Where would you look to find the correct spelling of *convenient?*

   Ⓐ a dictionary
   Ⓑ a magazine
   Ⓒ an encyclopedia
   Ⓓ an atlas

2. Where would you look to find a word that has the same meaning as the word *fierce?*

   Ⓕ an encyclopedia
   Ⓖ an atlas
   Ⓗ a thesaurus
   Ⓘ a dictionary

3. Where would you look to learn the countries in Africa?

   Ⓐ a thesaurus
   Ⓑ a magazine
   Ⓒ an atlas
   Ⓓ a dictionary

4. You are writing a report about Somalia. Where would you look to learn facts about the country's geography, history, and culture?

   Ⓕ an atlas
   Ⓖ a thesaurus
   Ⓗ a dictionary
   Ⓘ an encyclopedia

Use Reference Sources

© Harcourt • Grade 3

`98`

---

▲ Use the dictionary page below to answer each question.

*lettuce*                                        *light*

**let•tuce** (let′ əs) *n.* A plant grown for its edible leaves.

**li•brar•y** (lī′ brer′ ē) *n.* A place in which books and newspapers are kept for reading, reference, or lending.

**lie** (lī) *v.* **lay, lain, lying, lies 1.** To be or place oneself at rest; recline. **2.** To be placed on or supported by a flat surface. *The lake lies beyond the hills.* **3.** To occupy a position or place. *n.* A false statement. *v.* **lied, lying, lies** To make a false statement.

5. What are the guide words on this dictionary page?

   Ⓐ *lettuce* and *library*
   Ⓑ *lettuce* and *light*
   Ⓒ *lettuce* and *lie*
   Ⓓ *library* and *lie*

6. Which meaning of *lie* is used in the sentence below?

   **It is wrong to tell a lie.**

   Ⓕ to be or place oneself at rest; recline
   Ⓖ to occupy a position or place
   Ⓗ a false statement
   Ⓘ to make a false statement

Use Reference Sources

© Harcourt • Grade 3

`99`

TOTAL SCORE: _____ /6

# Robust Vocabulary

🔺 **Choose the word that best completes each sentence.**

Weekly
Lesson Test
Lesson 9

1. You should have seen my _____ when I made the team.
   - (A) curiosity
   - **(B) reaction**
   - (C) banquet
   - (D) gaze

2. The severe drought led to a _____ in the country.
   - (F) gaze
   - (G) banquet
   - (H) momentum
   - **(I) famine**

3. Because of the pleasant weather, I felt very _____.
   - **(A) agreeable**
   - (B) dense
   - (C) ferocious
   - (D) dominant

4. All we could do was _____ at the painting in the museum.
   - (F) flick
   - **(G) gaze**
   - (H) chatter
   - (I) dense

5. You should gather all the _____ you'll need.
   - (A) famine
   - (B) generous
   - **(C) ingredients**
   - (D) curiosity

Weekly
Lesson Test
Lesson 9

6. We became separated in the _____ forest.
   - **(F) dense**
   - (G) generous
   - (H) dominant
   - (I) agreeable

7. What food will you bring to the _____ this weekend?
   - (A) curiosity
   - (B) momentum
   - (C) reaction
   - **(D) banquet**

8. Mom was _____ and gave me an extra dollar.
   - (F) competent
   - **(G) generous**
   - (H) dense
   - (I) suspicious

9. As more people hear about it, the fundraiser gains _____.
   - (A) famine
   - (B) ingredients
   - **(C) momentum**
   - (D) reaction

10. Your curly purple wig is a _____.
    - (F) reaction
    - (G) momentum
    - (H) gaze
    - **(I) curiosity**

TOTAL SCORE: _____ /10

## Oral Reading Fluency

Today was rainy. Usually my sister and I complain to 10

our parents that we're bored. They usually come up with 20

a list of chores we could do so that we "won't be bored." 33

Well, that is not what happened today. 40

My sister and I were in her room complaining because 50

we wanted to play volleyball outside. My sister suggested 59

that we play inside. But, one of our main rules is that 71

there is to be no ball playing in the house. That rule came 84

after I broke a lamp with a softball. 92

We put our heads together and came up with a great 103

game using a balloon. We strung a piece of string across 114

the floor, just inches above the ground. We sat on the 125

floor, leaned back on our hands, and pushed up onto our 136

hands and feet. We would only be allowed to kick the 147

"ball" over the "net" with one foot. All three other limbs 158

had to stay on the floor. It was fun! So we invited two 171

friends over and had a great game of "foot-ball!" 180

_____ /WCPM

---

## Grammar: Singular and Plural Nouns

▲ Choose the word that correctly completes each sentence.

1. The athlete had two _____.
   - Ⓐ injury
   - Ⓑ injurys
   - Ⓒ injuries
   - Ⓓ injuryes

2. A mother fox and her baby _____ crossed the field.
   - Ⓕ foxs
   - Ⓖ foxes
   - Ⓗ foxies
   - Ⓘ foxys

3. I have lost only six _____.
   - Ⓐ tooth
   - Ⓑ tooths
   - Ⓒ teeth
   - Ⓓ teeths

4. What do you want to be doing in 20 _____?
   - Ⓕ year
   - Ⓖ years
   - Ⓗ yeares
   - Ⓘ yearses

TOTAL SCORE: _____ /4

## Selection Comprehension

▲ **Choose the best answer for each question.**

**1.** Which sentence BEST describes the problem in the play?

Ⓐ Mama Bear's pancakes taste better than Bananas'.

Ⓑ Cam and Sam need help from Evie Dense.

Ⓒ Bananas does not see the end of a movie.

Ⓓ Someone has broken into the Bears' home.

**2.** Why do the Bears go to see Cam and Sam?

Ⓕ to ask them for help

Ⓖ to invite them to breakfast

Ⓗ to complain about Bananas

Ⓘ to ask how to find Evie Dense

**3.** What can readers tell about Cam and Sam?

Ⓐ They have been to the Bears' house before.

Ⓑ They always work with Evie Dense.

Ⓒ They like to eat banana pancakes.

Ⓓ They are good at noticing clues.

**4.** How does Bananas feel when he sees the Bears at his door?

Ⓕ frightened

Ⓖ impatient

Ⓗ lucky

Ⓘ proud

**5.** What happens JUST AFTER Sam finds out the hairs are yellow yarn?

Ⓐ Mama Bear makes her famous pancakes.

Ⓑ Bananas tells Sam what really happened.

Ⓒ The Bears go to Cam's and Sam's office.

Ⓓ Cam and Sam go to the Bears' house.

**6.** How do Cam and Sam solve the mystery?

Ⓕ They use clues to determine what happened.

Ⓖ They get a call telling them who broke in.

Ⓗ They remember a case just like this one.

Ⓘ They see the thief taking food again.

**7.** Why did the author write this play?

Ⓐ to teach facts about bears

Ⓑ to get people to protect bears

Ⓒ to tell a funny story about bears

Ⓓ to warn that bears are dangerous

**8.** What is MOST LIKELY to happen next?

Ⓕ Bananas will move to the Bears' house.

Ⓖ The Bears and Bananas will eat pancakes.

Ⓗ Bananas will watch the end of the movie.

Ⓘ Cam and Sam will look for a yellow sweater.

## Robust Vocabulary

▶ Choose the word that best completes each sentence.

1. If you are guilty, you should _____.
   - (A) confess
   - (B) expert
   - (C) investigate
   - (D) gaze

2. The _____ on sea life talked to us about whales.
   - (F) banquet
   - (G) reaction
   - (H) laboratory
   - (I) expert

3. The comedian told a joke that was _____.
   - (A) various
   - (B) amusing
   - (C) perplexed
   - (D) inquisitive

4. I _____ that you will find your lost keys.
   - (F) alert
   - (G) confess
   - (H) suspect
   - (I) investigate

5. The police will _____ the crime.
   - (A) confess
   - (B) suspect
   - (C) alert
   - (D) investigate

---

READ
THINK
EXPLAIN

## Written Response (worth two points)

9. Explain why Cam and Sam make good detectives. Use details and information from "The Case of the Three Bears' Breakfast" to help you answer.

**Sample two-point response: They are good at finding**

**clues, and they do this work all the time.**

_____

_____

_____

Selection Comprehension
"The Case of the Three
Bears' Breakfast"
© Harcourt • Grade 3

106

TOTAL SCORE: _____ /8 + _____ /2

## Selection Comprehension

▲ **Choose the best answer for each question.**

**1.** How does Carolyn MOST LIKELY feel when she watches Dana and Josh in the show?

- (A) She does not care how they do.
- (B) She is angry they perform so well.
- (C) She wishes they would make a mistake.
- (D) She is proud but thinks she will do better.

**2.** Why does Carolyn forget the words when she goes onstage?

- (F) She has not practiced enough.
- (G) The kids are making too much noise.
- (H) She gets nervous in front of the crowd.
- (I) Greg asks her to switch poems with him.

**3.** Why does Mrs. Lasiter whisper "I am the river" from offstage?

- (A) She is telling Carolyn what to say.
- (B) She is practicing a children's song.
- (C) She is welcoming the audience.
- (D) She is making fun of Carolyn.

**4.** What is Carolyn's BIGGEST problem in the story?

- (F) She thinks Mama does not care about her enough.
- (G) She worries that Mrs. Lasiter does not like her.
- (H) She does not get to be first in the program.
- (I) She thinks the audience feels sorry for her.

Selection Comprehension
"Loved Best"
© Harcourt • Grade 3

109

---

**6.** Unable to solve the riddle, I was _____.

- (F) perplexed
- (G) inviting
- (H) ferocious
- (I) various

**7.** The scientist did an experiment in her _____.

- (A) expert
- (B) reaction
- (C) laboratory
- (D) signal

**8.** On a hot summer day, a swimming pool looks _____.

- (F) inquisitive
- (G) inviting
- (H) various
- (I) amusing

**9.** I packed _____ items in my suitcase, including sweaters and sunscreen.

- (A) various
- (B) inviting
- (C) perplexed
- (D) generous

**10.** After slowly approaching the basket, the _____ kitten jumped in.

- (F) various
- (G) amusing
- (H) perplexed
- (I) inquisitive

**Robust Vocabulary**

© Harcourt • Grade 3

108

**TOTAL SCORE:** _____ /10

---

5. How is Carolyn DIFFERENT just before and just after she goes onstage?

Ⓐ Before she is kind, but after she is mean.

Ⓑ Before she is afraid, but after she is brave.

Ⓒ Before she is ashamed, but after she is proud.

Ⓓ Before she is sure of herself, but after she is upset.

6. Why does Carolyn think she isn't the favorite child?

Ⓕ Mama tells Daddy she likes Dana the best.

Ⓖ Mama gives Dana and Josh special attention.

Ⓗ Mama thinks Dana was better in the program.

Ⓘ Mama says young children like Dana are cuter.

7. At the end of the story, how does Carolyn MOST LIKELY feel?

Ⓐ happy

Ⓑ helpful

Ⓒ selfish

Ⓓ confused

8. What is this story MOST LIKE?

Ⓕ a poem

Ⓖ a fairy tale

Ⓗ realistic fiction

Ⓘ historical fiction

---

READ
THINK
EXPLAIN

## Written Response (worth two points)

9. **COMPARING TEXTS** What did both Carolyn in "Loved Best" and the shepherd boy in "The Shepherd Boy and the Wolf" do that was the SAME? Use information and details from BOTH stories to support your answer.

**Sample two-point response:** Carolyn and the boy both

pretended something that wasn't true. Carolyn pretended

to be sick. The boy pretended a wolf was near. They both

just wanted attention.

## Phonics/Spelling: C-*le* Syllable

▲ Choose the correct way to divide each word into syllables.

**1.** title
  Ⓐ tit-le
  Ⓑ ti-tle
  Ⓒ titl-e
  Ⓓ t-itle

**2.** bundle
  Ⓕ bu-ndle
  Ⓖ bundl-e
  Ⓗ bun-dle
  Ⓘ bund-le

**3.** table
  Ⓐ ta-ble
  Ⓑ t-able
  Ⓒ tabl-e
  Ⓓ tab-le

**4.** topple
  Ⓕ topp-le
  Ⓖ to-pple
  Ⓗ t-opple
  Ⓘ top-ple

TOTAL SCORE: _____ /4

---

## Focus Skill: Plot

▲ Read the passage. Then choose the best answer for each question.

### Cereal and Milk for Breakfast

One Sunday, Isabel sat at the dinner table with her family. "Meatloaf?" she shrieked in horror. "I *hate* meatloaf. I *wanted* pizza."

"Isabel," said her mother, "you always want pizza! Eat your meatloaf."

"Wait a minute," said Isabel's dad. "I think Isabel should have what she wants. Let her eat pizza for breakfast, lunch, and dinner."

"Yes!" celebrated Isabel.

Monday and Tuesday were great! Isabel ate cheese pizza for breakfast, sausage pizza for lunch, and pepperoni pizza for dinner. On Wednesday, Isabel took a bowl from the cupboard. She took out cereal and began pouring it into the bowl. Her mother took it away and gave her a slice of cheese pizza. Isabel didn't know what to do. She'd asked for this. Now what would she do?

"Mom, I don't *want* pizza for breakfast," she complained. "I *want* cereal and milk."

"You wanted pizza, and you got pizza. That's all you can have to eat."

After soccer practice, the family sat down to eat dinner. Everyone had a plate of delicious ham and macaroni and cheese. "That smells so good!" said Isabel. At her place was a plate of pizza. Isabel couldn't stand to even look at it! She looked at her mom and said, "Mom, I apologize for being so rude! Thank you for cooking such wonderful meals. I would love to eat them."

---

Name _____

Mom got up from the table and returned with an extra plate. She loaded it with ham and macaroni and cheese and handed it to Isabel. Mom winked and asked with a smile, "What would you think of cereal and milk for breakfast tomorrow?"

1. What is Isabel's main problem in the story?
   Ⓐ She doesn't want to eat meatloaf.
   Ⓑ She can eat only pizza.
   Ⓒ She has an argument with her family.
   Ⓓ She doesn't want to help in the kitchen.

2. How does Isabel first try to solve her problem?
   Ⓕ She treats her family with respect.
   Ⓖ She refuses to eat meatloaf.
   Ⓗ She eats ham and macaroni and cheese.
   Ⓘ She gets out a bowl and cereal for breakfast.

3. What happens to Isabel during the story?
   Ⓐ She gets weary of eating pizza.
   Ⓑ She learns to cook.
   Ⓒ She joins a soccer team.
   Ⓓ She learns to try new foods.

4. How does Isabel solve her problem?
   Ⓕ She cooks her own food.
   Ⓖ She eats when her family is gone.
   Ⓗ She apologizes to her mother.
   Ⓘ She plays soccer at dinnertime.

**Focus Skill: Plot**

© Harcourt • Grade 3

114

---

Name _____

## Use Context Clues

▲ **Choose the best answer for each question.**

1. The sign warned us to be *cautious* when walking on the wet floor. What does *cautious* mean?
   Ⓐ awake
   Ⓑ careful
   Ⓒ dangerous
   Ⓓ brave

2. Reading glasses *magnify* small print. What does *magnify* mean?
   Ⓕ to make larger
   Ⓖ to be able to read
   Ⓗ to understand
   Ⓘ to give a reply

3. I was *furious* when I found out my friend hadn't told me the truth. What does *furious* mean?
   Ⓐ afraid
   Ⓑ unusually happy
   Ⓒ very angry
   Ⓓ brave

4. The teacher *demonstrated* how to make a model of a volcano. What does *demonstrated* mean?
   Ⓕ gave away
   Ⓖ held tightly
   Ⓗ questioned
   Ⓘ showed

**Use Context Clues**

© Harcourt • Grade 3

115

TOTAL SCORE: _____ /4

---

Name _____

## Robust Vocabulary

▲ Choose the word that best completes each sentence.

1. She _____ when she heard the bad news.
   - Ⓐ praised
   - Ⓑ perplexed
   - Ⓒ sobbed
   - Ⓓ astonished

2. He felt _____ when she received a gift that he wanted.
   - Ⓕ envious
   - Ⓖ brief
   - Ⓗ encouraging
   - Ⓘ soothing

3. The coach was _____ when we won the game.
   - Ⓐ inquisitive
   - Ⓑ envious
   - Ⓒ ferocious
   - Ⓓ astonished

4. The famous singer made a _____ stop to sign autographs.
   - Ⓕ dense
   - Ⓖ brief
   - Ⓗ soothing
   - Ⓘ perplexed

5. We _____ the puppy when it followed our command.
   - Ⓐ praised
   - Ⓑ swooned
   - Ⓒ astonished
   - Ⓓ sobbed

Robust Vocabulary

© Harcourt • Grade 3

117

---

Name _____

5. The letter was written on blue *stationery*. What does *stationery* mean?
   - Ⓐ desk
   - Ⓑ paper
   - Ⓒ ink
   - Ⓓ book

6. The new factory will *produce* computers. What does *produce* mean?
   - Ⓕ to make
   - Ⓖ to invent
   - Ⓗ to buy
   - Ⓘ to break

7. I made the *decision* to try out for the math team. What does *decision* mean?
   - Ⓐ guess
   - Ⓑ money
   - Ⓒ secret
   - Ⓓ choice

8. We got a *glimpse* of the boat as it zipped across the lake. What does *glimpse* mean?
   - Ⓕ stay away
   - Ⓖ soak with water
   - Ⓗ quick look
   - Ⓘ come near

Use Context Clues

© Harcourt • Grade 3

116

TOTAL SCORE: _____ /8

---

*Student Edition* pp. 116–117

© Harcourt • Grade 3

## Grammar: Possessive Nouns

▲ **Read each sentence. Choose the word that completes
the sentence.**

1. I found a _____ collar.
   - Ⓐ dogs
   - Ⓑ dog's
   - Ⓒ dogs's
   - Ⓓ dogs'

2. The two _____ closets were clean.
   - Ⓕ girls
   - Ⓖ girl's
   - Ⓗ girls'
   - Ⓘ girls's

3. Only one _____ leaves had turned colors.
   - Ⓐ tree
   - Ⓑ trees
   - Ⓒ trees'
   - Ⓓ tree's

4. We saw the _____ huge nests.
   - Ⓕ eagles'
   - Ⓖ eagles
   - Ⓗ eagle's
   - Ⓘ eagles's

Grammar: Possessive Nouns

© Harcourt • Grade 3

`119`

TOTAL SCORE: _____ /4

---

6. The baby stopped crying when he heard the
   _____ sound of his mother's voice.
   - Ⓐ inquisitive
   - Ⓑ chuckling
   - Ⓒ soothing
   - Ⓓ astonished

7. She was so nervous about the performance that she _____
   as she walked onto the stage.
   - Ⓐ astonished
   - Ⓑ swooned
   - Ⓒ perplexed
   - Ⓓ praised

8. The teacher's _____ words made me feel better.
   - Ⓕ encouraging
   - Ⓖ astonished
   - Ⓗ envious
   - Ⓘ chuckling

9. The child's _____ let us know the clown was funny.
   - Ⓐ rivalry
   - Ⓑ encouraging
   - Ⓒ soothing
   - Ⓓ chuckling

10. The brother and sister ended their _____.
    - Ⓕ suspect
    - Ⓖ rivalry
    - Ⓗ expert
    - Ⓘ brief

Robust Vocabulary

© Harcourt • Grade 3

`118`

TOTAL SCORE: _____ /10

---

***Student Edition** pp. 118–119*

`90`

Name _____

## Selection Comprehension

▲ Choose the best answer for each question.

1. Which sentence BEST tells what the story is about?
   - Ⓐ Max gets a pen pal and makes friends for others, too.
   - Ⓑ Max and a pen pal write about brothers and sisters.
   - Ⓒ Max decides to sneak a note into a box of grapes.
   - Ⓓ Max has many friends and a pony of his own.

2. How does Max get the idea of having a pen pal?
   - Ⓕ He reads about pen pals in a book.
   - Ⓖ His father used to have a pen pal.
   - Ⓗ His mother tells him he needs a new friend.
   - Ⓘ The packing house manager asks him a question.

3. How does Maggie get her first note from Max?
   - Ⓐ Ms. Moore gives it to her.
   - Ⓑ Don Manuel mails it to her.
   - Ⓒ Her father brings it home to her.
   - Ⓓ A friend at school gives it to her.

4. What is one way Max and Maggie are ALIKE?
   - Ⓕ Both speak Spanish.
   - Ⓖ Both have hobbies.
   - Ⓗ Both live on a fruit farm.
   - Ⓘ Both live in South America.

Selection Comprehension
"A Pen Pal for Max"
— © Harcourt • Grade 3

121

---

Name _____

## Oral Reading Fluency

| | |
|---|---|
| Our solar system used to have nine planets. Now it has | 11 |
| eight. In August 2006, scientists decided that Pluto was | 20 |
| not a planet at all. Pluto is very small. It is even smaller | 33 |
| than our moon. Pluto is also very far away from Earth. It | 45 |
| is so small and so far away that it is hard to see, even with | 60 |
| a telescope. No space probe has ever gone there. As a | 71 |
| result, scientists know very little about Pluto. | 78 |
| Since Pluto was discovered in 1930, scientists have | 86 |
| wondered whether it really is a planet. This is partly | 96 |
| because it is so small and so far away. Now scientists have | 108 |
| decided to answer the question. First they had to answer | 118 |
| another question. What is a planet? They found that all | 128 |
| the other planets have at least three things in common. | 138 |
| Pluto has only two of these things. Scientists decided to | 148 |
| give Pluto a new title, "dwarf planet." Dwarf planets, like | 158 |
| the other planets, go around the sun. They also have a | 169 |
| nearly round shape. | 172 |

_____ /WCPM

Oral Reading Fluency
© Harcourt • Grade 3

120

---

![READ THINK EXPLAIN]

## Written Response (worth two points)

9. Pretend that you are Max. Write what you would tell Maggie the next time you write to her. Use information and details from "A Pen Pal for Max" to support your answer.

**Sample two-point response: I would tell Maggie thank**

you for the presents she sent to our class. I would tell

her I was at Don Manuel's during the earthquake. We

ran outside. When it stopped trembling, I was glad to

get home to my family.

TOTAL SCORE: _____ /8 + _____ /2

---

5. What can readers tell about Maggie and her classmates?
   - (A) They are good at soccer.
   - (B) They want to visit Chile.
   - (C) They care about other people.
   - (D) They have been in an earthquake.

6. Why does Max take Maggie's letters to Don Manuel?
   - (F) He is afraid that Don Manuel is lonely.
   - (G) He needs help reading Maggie's English writing.
   - (H) He does not know what to write back to Maggie.
   - (I) He thinks Don Manuel should get his own pen pal.

7. What is MOST LIKELY to happen next?
   - (A) Max's class will travel to the United States.
   - (B) Don Manuel will take Max to meet Maggie.
   - (C) Max's teacher will give the boxes to Max's father.
   - (D) Children in Max's class will write to Maggie's class.

8. How can readers tell this story is realistic fiction?
   - (F) It takes place in a far-away country.
   - (G) The events could not really happen.
   - (H) The characters have feelings like real people.
   - (I) It tells about an important person from the past.

---

## Phonics/Spelling: Consonant Digraphs
### /n/kn, gn; /r/wr; /f/gh

▲ Read each model word. Then fill in the circle next to the word that has the same sound as the underlined part of the model word and completes each sentence.

**1. chief**

The funny joke made me _____.

- Ⓐ chuckle
- Ⓑ grief
- Ⓒ giggle
- Ⓓ laugh

**2. rock**

I wrote the _____ answer on the test.

- Ⓕ wrong
- Ⓖ same
- Ⓗ longest
- Ⓘ ready

**3. note**

The doctor _____ her name on the paper.

- Ⓐ knocked
- Ⓑ wrote
- Ⓒ signed
- Ⓓ saw

**4. nod**

Be careful with the sharp _____.

- Ⓕ gnat
- Ⓖ knife
- Ⓗ key
- Ⓘ file

Phonics/Spelling: Consonant Digraphs
/n/kn, gn; /r/wr; /f/gh
© Harcourt • Grade 3

124

TOTAL SCORE: _____ /4

---

## Focus Skill: Plot

▲ Read the passage. Then choose the best answer for each question.

### Taking Care of Muffy

Mia took the key from Mrs. Galloway and put it safely in the pocket of her jacket. "Goodbye," Mia said to Mr. and Mrs. Galloway. "Have a great trip and don't worry about Muffy. I'll take good care of her."

Because the Galloways were going on vacation, they had asked 16-year-old Mia to take care of their dog, Muffy, while they were gone. Mia loves playing with Muffy, so she agreed. The Galloways would pay Mia ten dollars for coming over before and after school every day to feed Muffy, take her outside, and play with her.

After dinner that night, Mia told her parents that she was going to take care of Muffy. As she walked next door, she reached into her pocket. She froze! Frantically, she searched her pocket, but the key was not there. What would she do? Mia could see Muffy through the window, wagging her tail, ready to play.

Mia walked to the front door. She turned the knob, but of course, it was locked. Mia looked in the grass. Had she dropped the key? The shiny metal was nowhere to be found.

Turning to go home, she ran into her mother. Mia opened her mouth to let her story spill out, but Mom interrupted her.

"Are you missing this?" she asked, holding up the key.

"Where did you find it?" Mia asked thankfully.

"I told you that we needed to sew that hole in your jacket pocket! Let's do that after you take care of Muffy."

"Yes," Mia agreed. "Let's do that!"

Focus Skill: Plot
© Harcourt • Grade 3

125

---

## Use Context Clues

▲ Choose the best answer for each question.

1. We went to the office of the new *physician*, Dr. Scott.
   What word helps you understand the meaning of *physician?*

   Ⓐ went
   Ⓑ office
   Ⓒ new
   ● Dr.

2. Even after we emptied the wastebasket, we could still smell the *rubbish*.
   What word helps you understand the meaning of *rubbish?*

   Ⓕ after
   Ⓖ emptied
   ● wastebasket
   Ⓘ smell

3. The schoolchildren learned about stars during the *astronomer's* brief speech.
   What word helps you understand the meaning of *astronomer?*

   Ⓐ schoolchildren
   ● stars
   Ⓒ brief
   Ⓓ speech

Use Context Clues

© Harcourt • Grade 3

---

1. What happens at the beginning of the story?

   Ⓐ Mia gets a new dog.
   ● Mia gets the key from the Galloways.
   Ⓒ Mia eats dinner with her family.
   Ⓓ Mia goes next door to play with Muffy.

2. What problem does Mia have?

   Ⓕ She forgets to take care of Muffy.
   Ⓖ She does not like dogs.
   ● She cannot find the key to her neighbor's house.
   Ⓘ She cannot earn enough money to get what she wants.

3. How is the problem solved?

   Ⓐ Mom brings the key to Mia.
   Ⓑ Mia remembers to take care of Muffy.
   Ⓒ Mia takes care of Muffy and earns ten dollars.
   Ⓓ Mom gets a dog for Mia.

4. Why does Mia lose something important?

   Ⓕ She isn't responsible.
   Ⓖ She usually loses things.
   Ⓗ She takes off her jacket.
   ● She has a hole in her pocket.

Focus Skill: Plot

© Harcourt • Grade 3

TOTAL SCORE: _____ /4

---

***Student Edition** pp. 126–127*

## Robust Vocabulary

▶ **Choose the word that best completes each sentence.**

1. John _____ the secret code.
   - Ⓐ mistaken
   - Ⓑ deciphered
   - Ⓒ astonished
   - Ⓓ fortunate

2. While I took the test, I found the hallway noise _____ .
   - Ⓕ bothersome
   - Ⓖ deciphered
   - Ⓗ heaving
   - Ⓘ mistaken

3. We didn't buy the car because it needed plenty of _____ .
   - Ⓐ encouraging
   - Ⓑ heaving
   - Ⓒ repairs
   - Ⓓ rivalry

4. Mom and I were _____ the annoying sales clerk.
   - Ⓕ mistaken
   - Ⓖ heaving
   - Ⓗ fortunate
   - Ⓘ dodging

5. Thomas thought he saw his teacher, but he was _____ .
   - Ⓐ bothersome
   - Ⓑ fortunate
   - Ⓒ mistaken
   - Ⓓ astonished

Robust Vocabulary

© Harcourt • Grade 3

`129`

---

4. You may have been able to trick me once, but you will not be able to *deceive* me again.
   What word helps you understand the meaning of *deceive?*
   - Ⓕ trick
   - Ⓖ once
   - Ⓗ able
   - Ⓘ again

5. The child is very *independent*. He wants to do everything on his own.
   What words help you understand the meaning of *independent?*
   - Ⓐ child, very
   - Ⓑ he wants to
   - Ⓒ very, everything
   - Ⓓ on his own

6. An octopus uses its *tentacles* to crawl along the ocean floor.
   What word helps you understand the meaning of *tentacles?*
   - Ⓕ octopus
   - Ⓖ crawl
   - Ⓗ along
   - Ⓘ ocean

**Use Context Clues**

© Harcourt • Grade 3

`128`

TOTAL SCORE: _____ /6

---

Name _____

## Grammar: Singular and Plural Pronouns

▲ Read each sentence. Choose the pronoun that
replaces the underlined word or words.

1. Lupe played tag with Kara at recess.

   Ⓐ she
   Ⓑ us
   Ⓒ her
   Ⓓ them

2. I will get the bike for you.

   Ⓕ it
   Ⓖ you
   Ⓗ its
   Ⓘ we

3. Omar and I have been friends since first grade.

   Ⓐ They
   Ⓑ Our
   Ⓒ My
   Ⓓ We

4. Where did you get the puppies?

   Ⓕ they
   Ⓖ them
   Ⓗ their
   Ⓘ it

Grammar: Singular and Plural Pronouns   131

© Harcourt • Grade 3

TOTAL SCORE: _____ /4

---

Name _____

6. Do you know how to _____ Spanish to English?

   Ⓕ din
   Ⓖ mistaken
   Ⓗ translate
   Ⓘ catastrophe

7. The _____ from the jet engine could be heard from far
   away.

   Ⓐ repairs
   Ⓑ din
   Ⓒ fortunate
   Ⓓ heaving

8. We were _____ to find two seats in the crowded theater.

   Ⓕ bothersome
   Ⓖ deciphered
   Ⓗ fortunate
   Ⓘ mistaken

9. The sailboats were _____ in the rough seas.

   Ⓐ din
   Ⓑ encouraging
   Ⓒ catastrophe
   Ⓓ heaving

10. The news of the _____ saddened us all.

    Ⓕ rivalry
    Ⓖ catastrophe
    Ⓗ repairs
    Ⓘ din

Robust Vocabulary   130

© Harcourt • Grade 3

TOTAL SCORE: _____ /10

---

## Selection Comprehension

▲ **Choose the best answer for each question.**

1. Why did the author write "A Tree Is Growing"?

   Ⓐ to explain how trees grow and change
   Ⓑ to describe one special kind of tree
   Ⓒ to teach how to take care of a tree
   Ⓓ to get people to plant more trees

2. How can readers tell "A Tree Is Growing" is expository nonfiction?

   Ⓕ It tells the author's personal feelings.
   Ⓖ It has a plot with a beginning, a middle, and an end.
   Ⓗ It has events that could not really happen.
   Ⓘ It has pictures and captions to explain ideas.

3. The article says the way trees grow is unusual because they grow taller

   Ⓐ only at the top.
   Ⓑ only in the spring.
   Ⓒ only from their roots.
   Ⓓ only when they are young.

4. People count tree rings to find out

   Ⓕ the kind of soil the tree needs.
   Ⓖ how long the tree will live.
   Ⓗ what kind of tree it is.
   Ⓘ the age of the tree.

---

## Oral Reading Fluency

| | |
|---|---:|
| If you have ever wished that you lived in a castle, keep | 12 |
| reading because you may soon change your mind! More | 21 |
| than a thousand years ago, royalty started constructing | 29 |
| stone castles because castles offered a safe place to live. | 39 |
| From the castle, people could protect their land from | 48 |
| enemies. Soldiers, servants, and animals lived inside the | 56 |
| castle, making it a bustling, crowded place. | 63 |
| It was frequently damp and cold inside the walls of | 73 |
| stone castles. Even in the summer time, the stone rooms | 83 |
| remained damp, causing people to spend as much time | 92 |
| outside the castle as possible. In the winter, cold winds | 102 |
| ripped through the rooms and hallways of a castle. | 111 |
| Rooms without a burning fire were quite cold. | 119 |
| Life in the castle was not very private because only | 129 |
| royalty had bedrooms and slept in beds. Most other | 138 |
| people slept in one large room called the great room on | 149 |
| benches or on the floor. Since most castles did not have | 160 |
| running water, people did not bathe every day. | 168 |
| Many castles remain standing today, but would you | 176 |
| want to live in one? | 181 |

_____ /WCPM

---

**Written Response** (worth two points)

READ
THINK
EXPLAIN

9. Explain how seeds are carried from place to place. Use information and details from "A Tree Is Growing" to support your answer.

Sample two-point response: When seeds fall to the

ground, animals carry them away. When they bury the

seeds, the seeds grow in a different place. Also, the

wind blows some seeds away. Some seeds float away

in the water.

---

5. How do insects help trees?

Ⓐ They carry water to the leaves.

Ⓑ They make food for the leaves.

Ⓒ They eat fallen leaves and make the soil better.

Ⓓ They keep the branches and the leaves clean.

6. What can people tell about an oak tree if its bark is rough and cracked?

Ⓕ The tree is old.

Ⓖ The tree needs minerals.

Ⓗ The tree is making sugar.

Ⓘ The tree lives in a warm climate.

7. Which fact BEST shows how strong tree roots are?

Ⓐ Roots carry minerals.

Ⓑ Roots can split a rock.

Ⓒ Roots hold a tree in place.

Ⓓ Roots soak up water from the ground.

8. The author uses the picture of the banyan tree roots to show

Ⓕ how roots act like pipelines.

Ⓖ how mushrooms grow among roots.

Ⓗ how some roots grow in an unusual way.

Ⓘ how roots spread out underground.

## Focus Skill: Author's Purpose

▲ **Read the passages. Then choose the best answer for each question.**

### Protect Your Head

Many people enjoy riding bikes. They ride for fun and for exercise. However, a fall from a bike is not fun. You can be hurt badly. That's why you should wear a bike helmet each time you ride a bike. When you wear a bike helmet, you lower your risk of brain injury. If you fall off your bike while wearing a helmet, you are almost 85 percent less likely to have a brain injury than if you were without a helmet. Be a smart bike rider, and wear a helmet each time you ride a bike.

1. What is the author's purpose?
   (A) to entertain readers with a story of a bike ride
   (B) to explain to readers how to ride a bike
   (C) to persuade readers to wear a bike helmet
   (D) to tell readers how to choose a bike helmet

2. Which sentence from the passage gives you a clue about the author's purpose?
   (F) Many people enjoy riding bikes.
   (G) They ride for fun and for exercise.
   (H) However, a fall from a bike is not fun.
   (I) When you wear a bike helmet, you lower your risk of brain injury.

---

## Phonics/Spelling: Consonants /s/c; /j/g, dge

▲ **Read each model word. Then fill in the circle next to the word that has the same sound as the underlined part of the model word and completes each sentence.**

1. soak
   Would you like more _____ to drink?
   (A) juice
   (B) music
   (C) dash
   (D) water

2. jump
   We parked the car in the _____.
   (F) join
   (G) garage
   (H) field
   (I) grass

3. badge
   Did you _____ the show?
   (A) choose
   (B) ledge
   (C) forget
   (D) enjoy

4. press
   We drove through the _____.
   (F) town
   (G) city
   (H) country
   (I) sharp

TOTAL SCORE: _____ /4

## A Good Fit

You know that you should wear a helmet when you ride a bicycle, but do you know how to choose the right one? Make sure that the helmet fits on top of your head and does not tip back. When you have the helmet on, you should have about a two-finger space between your eyebrows and the front of the helmet. When you buckle the helmet, the buckle should be snug when you open your mouth wide. Now you know how your helmet should fit. Be sure to wear it each time you ride.

3. What is the author's purpose in writing this selection?

Ⓐ to persuade readers to ride bikes safely

Ⓑ to inform readers how to choose a helmet

Ⓒ to entertain readers with a story about bike riding

Ⓓ to teach readers how to ride a bike while wearing a helmet

4. Why did the author include the last sentence?

Ⓕ to encourage readers to wear helmets

Ⓖ to describe the safest style of bike helmet

Ⓗ to show the best way to wear a bike helmet

Ⓘ to persuade readers to ride bikes

Focus Skill: Author's Purpose

138

---

## Use Graphic Aids

▲ Read the passage. Then choose the best answer for each question.

Most Americans drive cars to work. However, riding a bicycle to work instead of driving a car can help keep the air clean. Riding a bicycle is also a good form of exercise.

**How Americans Get to Work**

▲ Use the graphic aid to answer the questions.

1. What information is shown in the graphic aid?

Ⓐ the number of people in the United States who own cars

Ⓑ the percentage of Americans who drive to work

Ⓒ the total number of bicycles in the United States

Ⓓ the percentage of Americans who like to walk for exercise

Use Graphic Aids

139

TOTAL SCORE: _____ /4

---

## Robust Vocabulary

▲ **Choose the word that best completes each sentence.**

1. The man lives in the house with the _____ on the front porch.
   - (A) particles
   - (B) repairs
   - (C) catastrophes
   - (D) columns

2. The puppy _____ on the rope I held.
   - (F) praised
   - (G) tugged
   - (H) deciphered
   - (I) paused

3. We watched the sugar _____ in the water.
   - (A) absorb
   - (B) swoon
   - (C) dissolve
   - (D) translate

4. I think the _____ that dug through our trash was a raccoon.
   - (F) scavenger
   - (G) expertise
   - (H) self-sufficient
   - (I) din

5. The mother hen _____ her chicks from danger.
   - (A) translates
   - (B) paused
   - (C) praises
   - (D) protects

Robust Vocabulary

© Harcourt • Grade 3

141

---

2. According to the graphic aid, what percentage of people walk to work?
   - (F) 88%
   - (G) 2%
   - (H) 4%
   - (I) 3%

3. Which one would be a good form of exercise?
   - (A) riding a bike
   - (B) driving a car
   - (C) working at home
   - (D) taking the bus

4. What does the graphic aid help you understand?
   - (F) how Americans do their jobs
   - (G) how Americans get to work
   - (H) how Americans ride their bicycles
   - (I) how Americans spend their free time

**TOTAL SCORE: _____ /4**

Use Graphic Aids

© Harcourt • Grade 3

140

---

*Student Edition* pp. 140–141

**101**

## Grammar: Subject and Object Pronouns

▲ **Read each sentence. Choose the pronoun that
replaces the underlined word or words.**

1. Mr. Harris told <u>Sarah and Seth</u> to work together as
   partners.
   Ⓐ they
   Ⓑ you
   Ⓒ them
   Ⓓ we

2. <u>Aunt Marta</u> gave the present to my sister.
   Ⓕ She
   Ⓖ Her
   Ⓗ We
   Ⓘ It

3. <u>Ken</u> rode the bus to school.
   Ⓐ We
   Ⓑ Him
   Ⓒ Me
   **Ⓓ He**

4. That board game belongs to <u>Eric and me</u>.
   **Ⓕ us**
   Ⓖ we
   Ⓗ they
   Ⓘ you

**TOTAL SCORE:** _____ /4

---

6. There were plenty of bread _____ on the blanket
   after our picnic.
   Ⓕ columns
   **Ⓖ particles**
   Ⓗ repairs
   Ⓘ catastrophes

7. Dwayne learned to be _____ when he went to college.
   Ⓐ protects
   Ⓑ mistaken
   **Ⓒ self-sufficient**
   Ⓓ fortunate

8. The sound of the _____ leaves as the campers walked
   through the woods frightened the animals.
   **Ⓕ rustling**
   Ⓖ self-sufficient
   Ⓗ mistaken
   Ⓘ fortunate

9. I _____ to take a deep breath before I continued my
   speech.
   **Ⓐ paused**
   Ⓑ deciphered
   Ⓒ praised
   Ⓓ tugged

10. Paper towels will _____ the spill.
    Ⓕ dissolve
    Ⓖ swoon
    Ⓗ translate
    **Ⓘ absorb**

**Robust Vocabulary**

**TOTAL SCORE:** _____ /10

---

*Student Edition* pp. 142–143

## Oral Reading Fluency

Bingwen raced to the bulletin board and searched it                    9

for the cast list. He just knew that the music teacher had            21

picked him for the leading role in the play. He found his             33

name and ran his finger across the page to the list of                45

characters. Oh no! There must be a mistake. How could                 55

he get such a small part? Bingwen read the list more                  66

carefully. Leon, Bingwen's best friend, had received the              74

starring role. Leon hadn't even planned on trying out                 83

until Bingwen had encouraged him to do so.                            91

Bingwen decided that he wouldn't be in the play at all               102

if he couldn't be the star.                                          108

At lunch, Leon came up to Bingwen. Leon told                         117

Bingwen that he felt bad. He wanted to drop out of the               129

play so that Bingwen could have the lead role.                       138

At that moment, Bingwen realized that Leon was                       146

willing to give up the lead just to make him happy.                  157

Bingwen told Leon that he would make a great star and                168

that he couldn't wait to practice the play with him.                 178

_____ /WCPM

---

## Selection Comprehension

▲ Choose the best answer for each question.

1. Why did the author write "One Small Place in a Tree"?
   A to warn people not to make a hole in a tree
   B to tell how to heal a tree that has a hole in it
   C to show how a hole in a tree changes over time
   D to tell a story about an animal living in a tree

2. What is "One Small Place in a Tree" MOST LIKE?
   F a fantasy
   G a tall tale
   H historical fiction
   I expository nonfiction

3. Which happens FIRST to a tree that gets a hole?
   A Birds make a nest in the hole.
   B Squirrels store nuts in the tree.
   C Beetles make tunnels in the hole.
   D The tree begins to rot from disease.

4. Why does the author tell about the bear sharpening its
   claws on the tree?
   F to show how a hole begins
   G to show what bears like to do
   H to show that bears are strong
   I to show why bears need trees

5. How do timber beetles change a tree?
   - (A) They help patch holes in a tree.
   - (B) They make more holes in a tree.
   - (C) They keep birds away from a tree.
   - (D) They clean loose bark off a tree.

6. What is the MAIN reason a woodpecker would go to a tree with a hole?
   - (F) to stay cool
   - (G) to eat a meal
   - (H) to take a rest
   - (I) to sharpen its beak

7. During which season is someone MOST LIKELY to find a family of mice in a tree hole?
   - (A) winter
   - (B) spring
   - (C) summer
   - (D) fall

8. The author thinks that holes in trees are
   - (F) useless.
   - (G) calming.
   - (H) important.
   - (I) frightening.

---

READ
THINK
EXPLAIN

**Written Response** (worth two points)

9. Explain the ways a hole in a tree helps animals and insects. Use information and details from "One Small Place in a Tree" to support your answer.

Sample two-point response: When a tree gets a hole, beetles move in. They make tunnels and lay eggs there. Later, when the tree rots, the bark falls off and leaves a bigger hole. Animals and birds can live in the hole.

## Phonics/Spelling: V/CV and VC/V Syllable Patterns

▲ Choose the correct way to divide each word into syllables.

1. pilot
   - Ⓐ pil-ot
   - Ⓑ p-ilot
   - Ⓒ pi-lot
   - Ⓓ pilo-t

2. closet
   - Ⓕ clos-et
   - Ⓖ cl-oset
   - Ⓗ clo-set
   - Ⓘ c-loset

3. label
   - Ⓐ l-abel
   - Ⓑ lab-el
   - Ⓒ la-be-l
   - Ⓓ la-bel

4. tiger
   - Ⓕ tig-er
   - Ⓖ ti-ger
   - Ⓗ t-iger
   - Ⓘ ti-g-er

---

## Focus Skill: Author's Purpose

▲ Read the passages. Then choose the best answer for each question.

### Building a Bridge

My class has been studying different types of bridges. Yesterday, our teacher gave us a challenge: build a model of a suspension bridge, complete with cables. Our bridges had to be made with straws and support the weight of 10 pennies.

I thought the assignment would be a snap, so I went home and went to work. At first, I couldn't get my bridge to hold even five pennies. Then I discovered that dental floss was great for holding the straw cables together. I can hardly wait to show my teacher. My bridge held 15 pennies!

1. What is the author's main purpose?
   - Ⓐ to entertain with a story about building a bridge
   - Ⓑ to explain how to build a model of a suspension bridge
   - Ⓒ to persuade readers to build a model of a bridge with straws
   - Ⓓ to tell readers about different kinds of bridges

2. Why did the author include the last line?
   - Ⓕ to explain why the speaker was building a bridge
   - Ⓖ to describe the challenges the speaker faced
   - Ⓗ to show the speaker's success
   - Ⓘ to inform about the speaker's money

TOTAL SCORE: _____ /4

## Use Graphic Aids

▲ Read the passage. Then choose the best answer for each question.

A computer is a tool that helps people work. Today, computers are everywhere. Many people use them every day. They are so common that we sometimes do not even recognize that a computer is in use in some places. The chart below shows some of the places where people use computers. What other places are likely to have a computer?

| Place | Computer | Job |
|---|---|---|
| Grocery store | Cash register and scanner | Reads bar codes and adds prices |
| Bank | Automated teller machine (ATM) | Allows people to get money from their bank accounts |
| Home | TV/VCR/DVD | Plays programs |
| School | Personal computer | Keeps school records Provides students with access to information |
| Library | Library catalog | Locates books in the library |

1. What kind of computer would you use at a bank?
   Ⓐ library catalog
   Ⓑ personal computer
   Ⓒ automated teller machine
   Ⓓ cash register

---

### The Golden Gate Bridge

The Golden Gate Bridge is a well-known landmark in the United States. People around the world recognize the bridge when they see a picture of it. Hundreds of workers worked for four years to build the bridge. The first cars crossed the bridge in 1937.

The Golden Gate Bridge spans more than 4,000 feet of the San Francisco Bay. About 9 million people from all over the world visit the bridge each year. About 2 billion cars have crossed the bridge since it opened.

3. What is the author's purpose in writing this selection?
   Ⓐ to persuade readers to drive across the Golden Gate Bridge
   Ⓑ to teach readers how workers built the Golden Gate Bridge
   Ⓒ to entertain readers with a story about the Golden Gate Bridge
   Ⓓ to inform readers about the Golden Gate Bridge

4. What information did the author give in this passage?
   Ⓕ a description of the Golden Gate Bridge
   Ⓖ facts about the Golden Gate Bridge
   Ⓗ a list of well-known places in San Francisco
   Ⓘ names of famous bridges around the world

TOTAL SCORE: _____ /4

## Robust Vocabulary

▲ **Choose the word that best completes each sentence.**

1. The air in the swamp was _____.
   - (A) self-sufficient
   - (B) damp ●
   - (C) harmony
   - (D) mistaken

2. Each year, the owls _____ in that tree.
   - (F) sprout
   - (G) absorb
   - (H) roost ●
   - (I) glimpse

3. The baseball player _____ the ball with the bat.
   - (A) strikes ●
   - (B) absorbs
   - (C) suppose
   - (D) dissolves

4. The mouse found its way through the _____.
   - (F) spears
   - (G) harmony
   - (H) transformation
   - (I) maze ●

5. We learned about the caterpillar's _____ into a butterfly.
   - (A) harmony
   - (B) transformation ●
   - (C) maze
   - (D) column

2. How does a grocery store computer help workers?
   - (F) totals the price of items ●
   - (G) gives the customers money
   - (H) locates items in the store
   - (I) plays entertaining programs

3. What kind of a computer plays programs?
   - (A) cash register
   - (B) automated teller machine
   - (C) TV/VCR/DVD ●
   - (D) library catalog

4. How would you use a computer in a library?
   - (F) to store school records
   - (G) to get money
   - (H) to add prices
   - (I) to find a book ●

TOTAL SCORE: _____ /4

## Grammar: Pronoun-Antecedent Agreement

▲ Read each sentence. Choose the pronoun that
agrees with the underlined antecedent.

1. Matt and Luke invited Sarah to join ____ game.

    (A) they

    (B) their

    (C) them

    (D) his

2. Jennifer watched as ____ balloon floated away.

    (F) her

    (G) she

    (H) my

    (I) he

3. That book belongs to Benjamin. ____ bought it last week.

    (A) You

    (B) Him

    (C) It

    (D) He

4. Hannah and I are going to the game together. ____ are
    friends.

    (F) Them

    (G) They

    (H) We

    (I) Us

Grammar: Pronoun-Antecedent
Agreement
© Harcourt • Grade 3

TOTAL SCORE: ____ /4

155

---

6. I ____ that tonight we will eat dinner at our
    favorite restaurant.

    (F) suppose

    (G) dissolve

    (H) roost

    (I) sprout

7. Different kinds of seeds will ____ at different times.

    (A) roost

    (B) dissolve

    (C) sprout

    (D) suppose

8. Did you catch a ____ of the shooting star?

    (F) harmony

    (G) transformation

    (H) maze

    (I) glimpse

9. The choir sang in perfect ____.

    (A) glimpse

    (B) maze

    (C) harmony

    (D) transformation

10. The fisherman ____ fish while standing in the water.

    (F) roost

    (G) spears

    (H) sprout

    (I) suppose

Robust Vocabulary
© Harcourt • Grade 3

TOTAL SCORE: ____ /10

154

## Selection Comprehension

▲ **Choose the best answer for each question.**

1. Which sentence BEST tells what the script is about?

  (A) The staff chooses letters and answers for a magazine.

  (B) Smarty Jackson tells the best way to choose a book.

  (C) Lots of children have been writing to a magazine.

  (D) Healthy Hart gets a letter about video games.

2. Which sentence is an OPINION from the script?

  (F) The next letter is about friendship.

  (G) Now my family has to move.

  (H) I had to move to a new town last year.

  (I) Great job, everyone.

3. To which expert should you write to ask which foods are good to eat?

  (A) Book Buddy

  (B) Friend Lee

  (C) Healthy Hart

  (D) Smarty Jackson

4. How are all the experts the SAME?

  (F) All have moved to a new town.

  (G) All tell when to do homework.

  (H) All try to help other children.

  (I) All tell how to stay healthy.

Selection Comprehension
"Ask the Experts"
© Harcourt • Grade 3

157

---

## Oral Reading Fluency

| | |
|---|---|
| For the last two years, Nadeem has tried to convince | 10 |
| his mother that he was responsible enough to have a | 20 |
| dog. When she agreed, Nadeem and Mom went to the | 30 |
| animal shelter. Nadeem knew that he wanted a puppy. | 39 |
| He was already planning the games they would play. | 48 |
| At the shelter, Nadeem heard barking and whining. He | 57 |
| thought some of the dogs sounded sad. Nadeem was | 66 |
| surprised to see the rows and rows of cages. Some dogs | 77 |
| whined in the back of their cages. Some dogs just wanted | 88 |
| to play. They wagged their tails and watched hopefully as | 98 |
| Nadeem walked past. | 101 |
| Nadeem looked at each dog. There were all shapes, | 110 |
| sizes, ages, and colors. Yet all the dogs had one thing in | 122 |
| common: they needed a home. | 127 |
| Nadeem turned to Mom. "I've made my decision," he | 136 |
| said. | 137 |
| "Already?" questioned Mom. "You haven't even taken | 144 |
| one dog out to play." | 149 |
| Nadeem decided that instead of taking home one dog, | 158 |
| he would come to the shelter after school each day. He | 169 |
| would be a volunteer and play with all of the dogs. | 180 |

_____ /WCPM

Oral Reading Fluency
© Harcourt • Grade 3

156

---

5. Which expert could BEST tell how to get better grades at school?

Ⓐ Book Buddy

Ⓑ Friend Lee

Ⓒ Healthy Hart

Ⓓ Smarty Jackson

6. Why does each expert read a letter out loud?

Ⓕ so the whole staff can decide what to print

Ⓖ so the experts can practice speaking clearly

Ⓗ so the staff can decide if the answers are right

Ⓘ so all the experts can answer each of the questions

7. Why do the editors and staff decide to put all the letters in the magazine?

Ⓐ They have extra space to fill.

Ⓑ They think all the answers are helpful.

Ⓒ They don't want to hurt any expert's feelings.

Ⓓ They always print all the letters they receive.

8. What happens RIGHT AFTER the children decide to use all the letters?

Ⓕ Friend Lee tells how to make new friends.

Ⓖ They find one last letter from a student.

Ⓗ Smarty gives tips for doing homework.

Ⓘ Taylor says, "So let's get started."

**Selection Comprehension**
"Ask the Experts"
© Harcourt • Grade 3

158

---

READ
THINK
EXPLAIN

## Written Response (worth two points)

9. Which expert do you think gave the best answer? Tell why you think that answer was the best. Use information from "Ask the Experts" to support your answer.

Sample two-point response: Friend Lee gave the best

answer because he helped someone feel better.

_____

_____

_____

_____

**Selection Comprehension**
"Ask the Experts"
© Harcourt • Grade 3

159

TOTAL SCORE: _____ /8 + _____ /2

---

## Robust Vocabulary

🔺 **Choose the word that best completes each sentence.**

1. You should _____ a doctor if you feel ill.
   - (A) shudder
   - (B) consult
   - (C) devise
   - (D) dissolve

2. I found an old _____ of my favorite magazine.
   - (F) advice
   - (G) correspondence
   - (H) expertise
   - (I) issue

3. It is not _____ to be outside in the rain.
   - (A) sensible
   - (B) inquisitive
   - (C) luscious
   - (D) bothersome

4. The scary story made the boy _____ as he listened.
   - (F) consult
   - (G) recommend
   - (H) shudder
   - (I) devise

5. She volunteered her _____ to help the victims.
   - (A) correspondence
   - (B) issue
   - (C) advice
   - (D) expertise

Robust Vocabulary

6. The magazine offered good _____ for how to plant flowers.
   - (F) issue
   - (G) advice
   - (H) correspondence
   - (I) expertise

7. What book do you _____ that I read?
   - (A) devise
   - (B) shudder
   - (C) consult
   - (D) recommend

8. Our assignment is to _____ a plan to help the community.
   - (F) devise
   - (G) consult
   - (H) shudder
   - (I) glimpse

9. I couldn't wait to eat the _____ peach.
   - (A) bothersome
   - (B) sensible
   - (C) luscious
   - (D) inquisitive

10. I kept up a _____ with my best friend when I was traveling.
   - (F) correspondence
   - (G) expertise
   - (H) advice
   - (I) issue

Robust Vocabulary

TOTAL SCORE: _____ /10

## Selection Comprehension

▲ **Choose the best answer for each question.**

1. What is the children's BIGGEST problem in the story?

   Ⓐ They have let a bad visitor come inside the house.

   Ⓑ They wonder when their mother will come home.

   Ⓒ They are frightened because it is dark and windy.

   Ⓓ They all have to sleep in the same small bed.

2. Why does Shang ask questions when the wolf first comes to the door?

   Ⓕ Her mother told her what to say.

   Ⓖ She has always been a curious child.

   Ⓗ She does not believe it is her grandmother.

   Ⓘ Her sisters want to know more about the stranger.

3. Compared with her two younger sisters, Shang is

   Ⓐ prettier.

   Ⓑ meaner.

   Ⓒ weaker.

   Ⓓ wiser.

4. What is the MAIN reason the author wrote "Lon Po Po"?

   Ⓕ to tell an interesting story about a wolf

   Ⓖ to explain how wolves get their food

   Ⓗ to teach facts about how wolves live

   Ⓘ to show how to take care of a wolf

5. How does Shang MOST LIKELY feel when she sees the wolf's hairy face?

   Ⓐ lucky

   Ⓑ afraid

   Ⓒ bored

   Ⓓ calm

6. Why does Shang say she will pick gingko nuts for the wolf?

   Ⓕ She wants the wolf to live forever.

   Ⓖ She hopes the wolf will get full and leave.

   Ⓗ She worries that the wolf needs soft food to eat.

   Ⓘ She wants the wolf to let her go outside to safety.

7. How are Shang and the wolf ALIKE?

   Ⓐ Both have a low voice.

   Ⓑ Both try to trick someone.

   Ⓒ Both pretend to be sleepy.

   Ⓓ Both dress like an old woman.

8. How can readers tell "Lon Po Po" is a fairy tale?

   Ⓕ It takes place in the future.

   Ⓖ It tells the author's own feelings.

   Ⓗ It has events that could not really happen.

   Ⓘ It tells true facts about an important person.

## Phonics/Spelling: r-Controlled Vowel /ôr/or, ore, our, ar, oar

▶ Read each model word. Then fill in the circle next to the word that has the same sound as the underlined part of the model word and completes each sentence.

**1. course**

_____ you leave make sure you get your coat.

- Ⓐ When
- Ⓑ Before
- Ⓒ After
- Ⓓ Source

**2. bore**

The _____ shook the glass in the windows.

- Ⓕ core
- Ⓖ wind
- Ⓗ storm
- Ⓘ branches

**3. sport**

She _____ a flower in her hair.

- Ⓐ wore
- Ⓑ had
- Ⓒ fort
- Ⓓ placed

**4. board**

My winter coat kept me _____.

- Ⓕ roar
- Ⓖ dry
- Ⓗ happy
- Ⓘ warm

Phonics/Spelling: r-Controlled Vowel
/ôr/or, ore, our, ar, oar
© Harcourt • Grade 3

165

TOTAL SCORE: _____ /4

READ
THINK
EXPLAIN

## Written Response (worth two points)

9. How do you know that the wolf in the story is smart? Use details and information from "Lon Po Po" to support your answer.

**Sample two-point response: The wolf is smart because**

**he dresses up like an old woman to fool the daughters.**

**He always has fast answers to Shang's questions. He acts**

**surprised that their mother isn't home. He waits until**

**dusk to go to their house so they can't see him well.**

Selection Comprehension
"Lon Po Po"
© Harcourt • Grade 3

164

TOTAL SCORE: _____ /8 + _____ /2

3. How are the two brothers the same?

   Ⓐ Both like history class.

   Ⓑ Both like peanut butter and banana sandwiches.

   Ⓒ Both enjoy playing football.

   Ⓓ Both are tall.

4. How does Anthony look different from Eddie?

   Ⓕ Anthony has green eyes.

   Ⓖ Anthony has freckles.

   Ⓗ Anthony has dimples.

   Ⓘ Anthony has dark brown hair.

---

# Focus Skill: Compare and Contrast

▲ Read the story. Then choose the best answer for each question.

Anthony and his older brother Eddie aren't very much alike. Anthony is tall with bright red hair and green eyes. Eddie is short with dark brown hair and blue eyes. Both have freckles and dimples.

The boys are interested in different things as well. Anthony likes to play football. Eddie would rather spend his time reading than playing sports. In school, Anthony's favorite class is math. Eddie likes history.

No matter how different they are in other ways, the brothers agree about one thing: peanut butter and banana sandwiches. Both boys love to eat their favorite sandwich.

1. How do Anthony and Eddie look alike?

   Ⓐ Both are tall.

   Ⓑ Both have freckles.

   Ⓒ Both have red hair.

   Ⓓ Both have blue eyes.

2. How is Eddie different from Anthony?

   Ⓕ Eddie likes math.

   Ⓖ Eddie plays football.

   Ⓗ Eddie likes peanut butter and banana sandwiches.

   Ⓘ Eddie spends his time reading.

Name _____

## Prefixes and Suffixes

▲ **Choose the best answer for each question.**

1. Which word means *not clear?*

   (A) reclear
   (B) clearful
   (C) unclear
   (D) clearless

2. Which word means *full of power?*

   (F) repower
   (G) unpower
   (H) powerless
   (I) powerful

3. Which word means *without a spot?*

   (A) spotless
   (B) unspot
   (C) spotful
   (D) respot

4. Which word means *to do again?*

   (F) undo
   (G) redo
   (H) doless
   (I) doful

5. Which word means *full of hope?*

   (A) hopeless
   (B) unhope
   (C) hopeful
   (D) rehope

Name _____

6. Which word means *to visit again?*

   (F) revisit
   (G) visitless
   (H) visitful
   (I) unvisit

7. Which word means *not happy?*

   (A) happyless
   (B) rehappy
   (C) happyful
   (D) unhappy

8. Which word means *without care?*

   (F) recare
   (G) careless
   (H) careful
   (I) uncare

TOTAL SCORE: _____ /8

*Student Edition pp. 168–169*

**115**

Name _____

## Robust Vocabulary

▲ Choose the word that best completes each sentence.

1. The _____ man smiled and spoke politely to the crowd.
   (A) expertise
   (B) charming
   (C) brittle
   (D) rustling

2. When the pots and pans fell, they made quite a _____.
   (F) racket
   (G) dissolve
   (H) brittle
   (I) correspondence

3. Her _____ plan was to start a school-wide recycling program.
   (A) self-sufficient
   (B) brittle
   (C) ingenious
   (D) tender

4. When playing chess, you must _____ the other player.
   (F) disguise
   (G) racket
   (H) outwit
   (I) devise

5. Mary _____ herself by wearing a wig and glasses.
   (A) disguised
   (B) embraced
   (C) recommended
   (D) consulted

Name _____

6. The _____ fox sneaked into the farmer's henhouse.
   (F) charming
   (G) cunning
   (H) outwit
   (I) delighted

7. My grandmother and I _____ when she came to visit.
   (A) recommended
   (B) disguised
   (C) embraced
   (D) devised

8. The meat was _____, so it wasn't hard to cut.
   (F) tender
   (G) dissolve
   (H) ingenious
   (I) charming

9. The hard candy broke easily because it was _____.
   (A) ingenious
   (B) delighted
   (C) cunning
   (D) brittle

10. I could tell by her smile that she was _____ to see me.
    (F) cunning
    (G) delighted
    (H) brittle
    (I) tender

TOTAL SCORE: _____ /10

## Grammar: Adjectives

▲ **Read each sentence. Choose the word from each sentence that is an adjective.**

1. I have a doll with a red skirt.
   - Ⓐ I
   - Ⓑ doll
   - Ⓒ red
   - Ⓓ skirt

2. Diego counts three turtles on the beach.
   - Ⓕ Diego
   - Ⓖ three
   - Ⓗ turtles
   - Ⓘ beach

3. It was a warm day, so I left my sweater at home.
   - Ⓐ warm
   - Ⓑ day
   - Ⓒ sweater
   - Ⓓ home

4. Many people waited on the sidewalk for the parade to begin.
   - Ⓕ Many
   - Ⓖ waited
   - Ⓗ sidewalk
   - Ⓘ parade

TOTAL SCORE: _____ /4

Grammar: Adjectives

172

---

## Oral Reading Fluency

Lisa was trying to solve a mystery. Whenever she — 9
bought cheese, it was gone within a few days. She had — 20
no idea where it went. — 25

"Perhaps I'm a sleepwalker, and I eat cheese in the — 35
night," thought Lisa. — 38

What Lisa did not know was that her cat, Louis, was — 49
also a great lover of cheese. Louis's family came from — 59
France. Cheese is very popular in France. Louis was also — 69
fond of grapes and fine bread. These things were hard for — 80
him to find in Lisa's house. — 86

Louis made every effort to keep his habit a secret, but — 97
Lisa discovered him eating a large piece of cheddar one — 107
night when she got up to get a glass of water. — 118

When Lisa turned on the light, she saw a piece of — 129
cheese on the floor. She spotted crumbs in Louis's — 138
whiskers. Louis was afraid that Lisa would be angry. — 147
Instead, she reached down to pet the cat. "We solved the — 158
cheese mystery!" she told Louis. He purred happily and — 167
went back to finish the last bit of cheddar. — 176

_____ /WCPM

Oral Reading Fluency

173

---

*Student Edition pp. 172–173*

**117**

## Selection Comprehension

▲ Choose the best answer for each question.

1. How can readers tell that "Two Bear Cubs" is a play?

(A) It gives information and facts about a subject.

(B) It tells a story and has words that sound alike.

(C) It has scenes and tells where characters are on a stage.

(D) It tells about real people and events that really happened.

2. What is the two bear cubs' BIGGEST problem in the story?

(F) They go where they are not supposed to go.

(G) They will not stop playing in the water.

(H) They scare away all the fish.

(I) They eat too many berries.

3. Compared with Younger Brother, Older Brother is more

(A) calm.

(B) careful.

(C) naughty.

(D) obedient.

4. The two bear cubs get trapped because the rock they are on

(F) floats away down the river.

(G) gets carried off by a hawk.

(H) becomes too hot and sunny.

(I) grows much bigger and higher.

5. How are Fox, Badger, Mother Deer, Mountain Lion, and Hawk ALIKE?

(A) All try to be helpful.

(B) All are grinding acorns.

(C) All carry loads of firewood.

(D) All are building new homes.

6. What is the MAIN reason the animals laugh when Measuring Worm says he will try to save the cubs?

(F) They think his name sounds silly.

(G) They think he is too little to help.

(H) They think his bright colors look funny.

(I) They think the way he moves is strange.

7. Which action BEST shows that Measuring Worm is brave?

(A) He cries "Tu-tok! Tu-tok! Tu-tok!"

(B) He calls "Wake up" to the two cubs.

(C) He keeps climbing even when he is afraid.

(D) He stops to see how much higher he must go.

8. What MOST helps Measuring Worm save the cubs?

(F) his strength

(G) his courage

(H) his speed

(I) his size

Name _____

## Phonics/Spelling: r-Controlled Vowel /ûr/er, ir, ur, or, ear

🔺 Read each model word. Then fill in the circle next to the word that has the same sound as the underlined part of the model word and completes each sentence.

**1. answer**

The picnic we had today was _____.

- Ⓐ fun
- Ⓑ perfect ●
- Ⓒ enjoyable
- Ⓓ heard

**2. hurt**

She wore a _____ ring.

- Ⓕ shirt
- Ⓖ gold
- Ⓗ pearl ●
- Ⓘ ruby

**3. word**

Tamika realized that she had forgotten her _____.

- Ⓐ purse ●
- Ⓑ bag
- Ⓒ torn
- Ⓓ umbrella

**4. girl**

The _____ helped customers choose their purchases.

- Ⓕ waitress
- Ⓖ bird
- Ⓗ boss
- Ⓘ clerk ●

---

Name _____

READ
THINK
EXPLAIN

## Written Response (worth two points)

9. Explain how Older Brother and Younger Brother are DIFFERENT. Use information and details from "Two Bear Cubs" to help you explain.

Sample two-point response: Older Brother is greedy and

eats the berries he's supposed to gather. He ignores

what his mother says and goes downriver when he isn't

supposed to. Younger Brother wants to do what their

mother says, but he always ends up copying Older

Brother.

_____

_____

## Focus Skill: Compare and Contrast

▲ **Read the story. Then choose the best answer for each question.**

Silas was a puppy the first time we took him to see the fireworks on the Fourth of July. Lukas, our older dog, went with us every year. We thought that Silas would enjoy the fireworks, just as Lukas always did.

Boy, were we wrong! Silas hated the fireworks. Actually, he was afraid of them. I think the loud noise and the bright lights confused him. He barked at the sky and then sat on the blanket, shaking. We felt terrible as we comforted him.

Years later, when Silas was older, we decided to try again. We packed a picnic and headed into town to see the fireworks with Lukas and Silas on their leashes. This time, Silas didn't seem to mind the fireworks. In fact, he sat next to Lukas happily and wagged his tail through the show.

1. How was Lukas different from Silas at the beginning of the story?
   - Ⓐ He was afraid of loud noises.
   - Ⓑ He was a puppy.
   - Ⓒ He barked at the sky.
   - Ⓓ He enjoyed the fireworks.

2. How had Silas changed the second time he went to see the fireworks?
   - Ⓕ He was older.
   - Ⓖ He hated the fireworks.
   - Ⓗ He was younger.
   - Ⓘ He shook with fear.

Focus Skill: Compare and Contrast

178

© Harcourt • Grade 3

3. How did Silas's feelings about the fireworks change?
   - Ⓐ He grew to dislike the fireworks.
   - Ⓑ His feelings did not change.
   - Ⓒ He grew to like the fireworks.
   - Ⓓ He became afraid of the fireworks.

4. What did Lukas and Silas have in common at the end of the story?
   - Ⓕ They were confused by the bright lights.
   - Ⓖ They enjoyed watching the fireworks.
   - Ⓗ They were both puppies.
   - Ⓘ They both barked at the sky.

Focus Skill: Compare and Contrast

179

© Harcourt • Grade 3

TOTAL SCORE: _____ /4

Name _____

## Prefixes and Suffixes

▲ Choose the best answer for each question.

**1.** Which word means *smaller than anyone else?*

Ⓐ small
Ⓑ smally
Ⓒ smallest
Ⓓ dissmall

**2.** Which word means *the most loud?*

Ⓕ loudest
Ⓖ disloud
Ⓗ loudly
Ⓘ louder

**3.** Which word means *to not agree?*

Ⓐ disagree
Ⓑ agreely
Ⓒ agreest
Ⓓ agreer

**4.** Which word means *to do something in a quiet way?*

Ⓕ quieter
Ⓖ quietly
Ⓗ quiestest
Ⓘ disquiet

Prefixes and Suffixes

© Harcourt • Grade 3

180

---

Name _____

**5.** Which word means *to not like?*

Ⓐ likely
Ⓑ likest
Ⓒ liker
Ⓓ dislike

**6.** Which word means *to do something in a happy way?*

Ⓕ happily
Ⓖ happiest
Ⓗ dishappy
Ⓘ happier

**7.** Which word means *the most soft?*

Ⓐ softer
Ⓑ softest
Ⓒ softly
Ⓓ dissoft

**8.** Which word means *more nice than someone?*

Ⓕ nicest
Ⓖ nicer
Ⓗ nicely
Ⓘ disnice

TOTAL SCORE: _____ /8

Prefixes and Suffixes

© Harcourt • Grade 3

181

---

# Robust Vocabulary

▲ **Choose the word that best completes each sentence.**

1. I went to bed late last night, and now I feel _____.

   (A) heroic
   (B) commendable
   (C) drowsy
   (D) cunning

2. Jamal knew that the test would require all of his _____.

   (F) awe
   (G) concentration
   (H) burden
   (I) dilemma

3. Tim tried to _____ his sister when she was upset.

   (A) outwit
   (B) scolding
   (C) console
   (D) disguise

4. Saving that kitten from the fire was a _____ act.

   (F) drowsy
   (G) burden
   (H) cunning
   (I) heroic

5. The teacher was _____ a student for being late to class.

   (A) scolding
   (B) consulting
   (C) glancing
   (D) devising

6. I am in _____ of your amazing baseball card collection.

   (F) concentration
   (G) dilemma
   (H) awe
   (I) burden

7. Rochelle kept _____ at her watch because she was late.

   (A) scolding
   (B) glancing
   (C) devising
   (D) consulting

8. Simon faced a _____ when trying to decide what to wear.

   (F) dilemma
   (G) drowsy
   (H) burden
   (I) concentration

9. It is _____ to pick up trash around the school.

   (A) heroic
   (B) drowsy
   (C) cunning
   (D) commendable

10. Carrying the large pack was a _____ for Carol during the hike.

    (F) concentration
    (G) burden
    (H) console
    (I) dilemma

TOTAL SCORE: _____ /10

## Grammar: Adjectives that Compare

▶ Read each sentence. Choose the correct form of the adjective to complete each sentence.

1. My room is _____ than my sister's.
   - (A) cleaner
   - (B) cleanest
   - (C) most clean
   - (D) more cleaner

2. Sue is the _____ person I have ever met.
   - (F) interestinger
   - (G) interestingest
   - (H) more interesting
   - (I) most interesting

3. Juan is _____ than Fred.
   - (A) considerater
   - (B) consideratest
   - (C) more considerate
   - (D) most considerate

4. Jim is the _____ runner on the track team.
   - (F) faster
   - (G) fastest
   - (H) more fast
   - (I) most fast

Grammar: Adjectives that Compare      184

TOTAL SCORE: _____ /4

© Harcourt • Grade 3

---

## Oral Reading Fluency

| | |
|---|---:|
| It was Denzel's first day working at the zoo, and | 10 |
| he was excited. Denzel's first task would be to follow | 20 |
| different workers around the zoo to learn about their | 29 |
| jobs. The first person he would work with was Melissa, | 39 |
| who worked in the reptile house—one of Denzel's favorite | 49 |
| spots in the zoo. | 55 |
| Denzel and Melissa spent most of the morning | 63 |
| feeding the snakes. Denzel learned all the snakes' names | 72 |
| and which foods they best liked to eat. | 80 |
| When they got to the cage of Ike, the boa constrictor, | 91 |
| Melissa looked worried. Neither she nor Denzel could see | 100 |
| the snake. | 102 |
| "Oh no! Is Ike gone?" Melissa said. | 109 |
| Denzel looked through the glass and agreed that the | 118 |
| snake *did* seem to be missing. "Where on earth could he | 129 |
| be?" Denzel wondered aloud. Ike was awfully large to | 138 |
| have just disappeared. | 141 |
| Just then, something caught Denzel's eye—a flash of | 150 |
| brown under a log in the cage. "I think I've solved the | 162 |
| mystery," Denzel said, pointing to the well-hidden snake. | 170 |
| He and Melissa both breathed a sigh of relief. | 179 |

_____ /WCPM

Oral Reading Fluency      185

© Harcourt • Grade 3

---

**Student Edition** pp. 184–185

123

5. What is one way Uncle Romie and James are ALIKE?
   - Ⓐ Both like baseball.
   - Ⓑ Both have an art show.
   - Ⓒ Both have deep voices.
   - Ⓓ Both live in New York.

6. Which is the BEST title for the birthday gift James makes for Uncle Romie?
   - Ⓕ "Uncle Romie's Favorite Things"
   - Ⓖ "Uncle Romie's Art Show"
   - Ⓗ "New York Trains"
   - Ⓘ "Beautiful Flowers"

7. Which sentence BEST tells a lesson James learns in the story?
   - Ⓐ People everywhere have the same feelings.
   - Ⓑ A problem should be solved quickly.
   - Ⓒ Work should be done before play.
   - Ⓓ People judge you by your friends.

8. How can readers tell "Me and Uncle Romie" is historical fiction?
   - Ⓕ It has words that rhyme.
   - Ⓖ It has events that could not happen.
   - Ⓗ It tells characters where to be on a stage.
   - Ⓘ It tells about people and places in the past.

Selection Comprehension
"Me and Uncle Romie"
© Harcourt • Grade 3

---

## Selection Comprehension

▲ Choose the best answer for each question.

1. Why is James worried about staying with Uncle Romie?
   - Ⓐ Uncle Romie has a lot of rules.
   - Ⓑ Uncle Romie does not like children.
   - Ⓒ Uncle Romie does not want a visitor.
   - Ⓓ Uncle Romie looks scary in his picture.

2. What is James's BIGGEST problem in the story?
   - Ⓕ He thinks his aunt will not like him.
   - Ⓖ He is nervous about riding on a train.
   - Ⓗ He thinks he may not have a good birthday.
   - Ⓘ He worries about his new brother and sister.

3. What can readers tell about Aunt Nanette?
   - Ⓐ She is bossy.
   - Ⓑ She cares about others.
   - Ⓒ She gets bored quickly.
   - Ⓓ She likes to tease people.

4. Based on the story, how is life the SAME in Harlem and in North Carolina?
   - Ⓕ People live in tall buildings.
   - Ⓖ People shop only in fancy stores.
   - Ⓗ People are friendly to each other.
   - Ⓘ People cook on the rooftops.

Selection Comprehension
"Me and Uncle Romie"
© Harcourt • Grade 3

---

## Phonics/Spelling: Suffixes -er, -est, -ly, -ful

▲ **Choose the word that correctly completes each sentence.**

1. The teacher has the _____ chair of all.
   - (A) largest
   - (B) larger
   - (C) largely
   - (D) large

2. Your pet bird seems _____ than mine.
   - (F) nice
   - (G) nicest
   - (H) nicely
   - (I) nicer

3. I am _____ that I did well on our reading test.
   - (A) thank
   - (B) thanks
   - (C) thankful
   - (D) thanked

4. Juanita _____ played with her new puppy.
   - (F) happy
   - (G) happily
   - (H) happiest
   - (I) happier

TOTAL SCORE: _____ /4

---

READ
THINK
EXPLAIN

## Written Response (worth two points)

9. How do James's feelings about Uncle Romie change in the story? Use information and details from "Me and Uncle Romie" to support your answer.

**Sample two-point response: At first, James is afraid of**

his uncle. Later, he learns that he has a lot in common

with him, like eating pepper jelly, watching trains, and

playing baseball. Then he loves his uncle and isn't afraid

of him.

TOTAL SCORE: _____ /8 + _____ /2

## Focus Skill: Theme

▲ **Read the story. Then choose the best answer for each question.**

Bess was an upset alligator. She was upset because her lake was dirty and filled with trash. This trash was making her friends who lived in the lake sick.

First, there was Kip and his family, a group of fish who were sick from swimming in the dirty water. Bess's pal Gus, a frog, had been sneezing for weeks. Her snake friend Sal had been home sick for ages. And come to think of it, Bess was feeling a bit ill herself.

As Bess looked around the lake, she could see empty cans, bottles, and other kinds of trash. She decided that feeling upset wasn't going to help Kip, Gus, or Sal. Cleaning the lake might help, though. She would start trying to make their home a cleaner place to live.

1. What is Bess's problem?
   - Ⓐ She has been sneezing for weeks.
   - Ⓑ The lake is too crowded with animals.
   - Ⓒ Trash in the lake is making her friends sick.
   - Ⓓ She has nowhere to throw her trash.

2. How does Bess decide to solve her problem?
   - Ⓕ She decides to move to another lake.
   - Ⓖ She decides to take care of Kip and Gus.
   - Ⓗ She decides to become a doctor.
   - Ⓘ She decides to clean the lake.

Focus Skill: Theme

© Harcourt • Grade 3

`190`

3. What is the theme of the story?
   - Ⓐ Friends spend time together.
   - Ⓑ Recycling helps keep Earth clean.
   - Ⓒ Solving problems is more helpful than being upset.
   - Ⓓ Different kinds of animals live in lakes.

4. What does the author seem to believe about litter?
   - Ⓕ The author believes that litter harms animals.
   - Ⓖ The author believes that litter is unavoidable.
   - Ⓗ The author believes that litter belongs in lakes.
   - Ⓘ The author believes that litter affects snakes most.

TOTAL SCORE: _____ /4

Focus Skill: Theme

© Harcourt • Grade 3

`191`

Name _____

## Follow Directions

▲ Read each question. Then choose the best answer
for each question.

Have you ever given a dog a bath? Giving a dog a bath can be
fun, but it is also a big responsibility. Follow these directions to
give your dog a bath.

First, collect all the materials you will need and place them
next to the sink or tub. You will need a brush, pet shampoo, and
clean towels. If you want to wash the dog's face, you will need
cotton balls and a washcloth.

Second, before you get the dog wet, test the temperature of
the water. Make sure it isn't too hot. Then, as you wash the dog,
be careful not to get shampoo or water in the dog's ears and
eyes. You can put cotton balls in the dog's ears to keep the water
out. Just be sure to remember to remove them when you are
done. Use the washcloth to clean around the dog's face.

Next, make sure you rinse all of the shampoo from the dog's
coat. Finally, use a clean towel to dry the dog thoroughly and a
brush to make the dog's coat neat and smooth.

1. What is step one?

   A Use a clean towel to dry the dog.

   B Collect the materials you will need.

   C Put cotton balls in the dog's ears.

   D Test the temperature of the water.

---

Name _____

2. What is step two?

   F Rinse all of the shampoo out of the dog's coat.

   G Brush the dog's coat to make it smooth.

   H Test the temperature of the water.

   I Use a washcloth around the dog's face.

3. Which of these is a time-order word?

   A follow

   B collect

   C next

   D learn

4. Which word lets you know that you are reading the last
   step?

   F second

   G next

   H first

   I finally

TOTAL SCORE: _____ /4

## Robust Vocabulary

▲ Choose the word that best completes each sentence.

1. I _____ the pudding when I dropped it on the floor.
   - Ⓐ yanked
   - Ⓑ glanced
   - Ⓒ ruined
   - Ⓓ scolded

2. The museum put the _____ in a glass case to protect it.
   - Ⓕ memory
   - Ⓖ masterpiece
   - Ⓗ heritage
   - Ⓘ burden

3. You should polish your medal because it looks _____.
   - Ⓐ glorious
   - Ⓑ drowsy
   - Ⓒ dull
   - Ⓓ commendable

4. My brother is so much taller than I that he _____ over me.
   - Ⓕ ruined
   - Ⓖ embraces
   - Ⓗ disguises
   - Ⓘ towers

5. The trip we took last year stands out in my _____.
   - Ⓐ memory
   - Ⓑ racket
   - Ⓒ dilemma
   - Ⓓ burden

6. The sunset over the ocean was a _____ sight.
   - Ⓕ dull
   - Ⓖ commendable
   - Ⓗ glorious
   - Ⓘ drowsy

7. The cat _____ silently behind the mouse.
   - Ⓐ disguised
   - Ⓑ crept
   - Ⓒ cunning
   - Ⓓ roost

8. It hurt when you accidentally _____ my hair.
   - Ⓕ yanked
   - Ⓖ ruined
   - Ⓗ crept
   - Ⓘ consoled

9. My family scrapbook teaches me about my _____.
   - Ⓐ burden
   - Ⓑ heritage
   - Ⓒ masterpiece
   - Ⓓ memory

10. I saw the lightning _____ across the sky.
   - Ⓕ streak
   - Ⓖ scold
   - Ⓗ towers
   - Ⓘ glance

TOTAL SCORE: _____ /10

## Oral Reading Fluency

| | |
|---|---|
| Gus loved being a clown in the circus. He enjoyed | 10 |
| making children laugh. No one could make a better | 19 |
| balloon animal than Gus. Even though he loved his job, | 29 |
| Gus was looking forward to his vacation. He decided to | 39 |
| go to an amusement park on his first day off because he | 51 |
| loved riding roller coasters. | 55 |
| Gus woke up early so that he could try his favorite | 66 |
| rides before the lines became too long. At first, he was | 77 |
| very sleepy. But, as he entered the park gates, all the | 88 |
| sights and sounds of the amusement park woke him up. | 98 |
| Gus had a great time all day, yet he was puzzled by the | 111 |
| way some people acted. Children kept coming up to him | 121 |
| to ask for balloons. Could they somehow guess that he | 131 |
| was a clown, even though he was on vacation? | 140 |
| When he got home, Gus looked in a mirror for the first | 152 |
| time all day. He saw that he had gone to the park dressed | 165 |
| in his clown costume! His sleepiness that morning must | 174 |
| have caused him to put it on by accident! | 183 |

_____ /WCPM

---

## Grammar: Articles

▲ **Read each sentence. Choose the article in each sentence.**

1. I watched butterflies fly around the garden.
   - Ⓐ I
   - Ⓑ watched
   - Ⓒ fly
   - Ⓓ the ●

2. I gave my brother a copy of his favorite book for his birthday.
   - Ⓕ my
   - Ⓖ a ●
   - Ⓗ of
   - Ⓘ his

3. I took an apple to my teacher last Tuesday.
   - Ⓐ I
   - Ⓑ an ●
   - Ⓒ to
   - Ⓓ last

4. My teacher asked me to get a pencil from my bag.
   - Ⓕ asked
   - Ⓖ me
   - Ⓗ to
   - Ⓘ a ●

TOTAL SCORE: _____ /4

Name _____

## Selection Comprehension

▲ Choose the best answer for each question.

1. How can readers tell that "Half-Chicken" is a folktale?
   - (A) It has maps and charts to teach about a subject.
   - (B) It is an old story that has been told many times.
   - (C) It has headings and words printed in a box.
   - (D) It tells about a real person from the past.

2. Which idea does this story explain?
   - (F) why roosters crow
   - (G) why chickens sit on eggs
   - (H) why chickens have feathers
   - (I) why weather vanes look like roosters

3. Half-Chicken is special MAINLY because of
   - (A) the way he looks.
   - (B) the way he sounds.
   - (C) the things he does.
   - (D) the things he says.

4. What happens JUST AFTER Half-Chicken gets to the palace?
   - (F) Half-Chicken finds a blocked stream.
   - (G) One of the guards laughs at Half-Chicken.
   - (H) Half-Chicken finds the wind tangled in bushes.
   - (I) The fire asks Half-Chicken to stay a while.

Selection Comprehension
"Half-Chicken"
© Harcourt • Grade 3

198

Name _____

5. Why do fire, water, and wind help Half-Chicken escape from the cook?
   - (A) because the cook is their enemy
   - (B) because the guards order them to help
   - (C) because Half-Chicken once helped them
   - (D) because they feel sorry for Half-Chicken

6. How can Half-Chicken BEST be described?
   - (F) silent
   - (G) greedy
   - (H) helpful
   - (I) complaining

7. Which lesson can be learned from this story?
   - (A) Help others, and they will help you.
   - (B) Do not be afraid to say, "I'm sorry."
   - (C) Always share if you have plenty.
   - (D) Never tell a secret to a friend.

8. How are the stream, the fire, and the wind ALIKE?
   - (F) All are blocked with branches.
   - (G) All are tangled in the bushes.
   - (H) All need to be fanned.
   - (I) All ask to be helped.

Selection Comprehension
"Half-Chicken"
© Harcourt • Grade 3

199

*Student Edition* pp. 198–199

## Phonics/Spelling: Prefixes *un-, re-, dis-*

▲ Choose the best answer for each question.

1. Which word means *not happy?*
   - Ⓐ unhappy
   - Ⓑ happier
   - Ⓒ happiest
   - Ⓓ happily

2. Which word means *do again?*
   - Ⓕ undo
   - Ⓖ doing
   - Ⓗ redo
   - Ⓘ did

3. Which word means *the opposite of appear?*
   - Ⓐ reappear
   - Ⓑ appears
   - Ⓒ appearing
   - Ⓓ disappear

4. Which word means *not safe?*
   - Ⓕ safest
   - Ⓖ unsafe
   - Ⓗ safer
   - Ⓘ safely

---

READ
THINK
EXPLAIN
### Written Response (worth two points)

9. **COMPARING TEXTS** How can you tell that the events in "Half-Chicken" and "I Sailed on Half a Ship" could not really happen? Use information and details from the story AND the poem to help you explain.

Sample two-point response: A chicken or a whale

couldn't live with only half a body. You couldn't

catch half a fish or tell time with half a clock. Fire,

wind, and water can't talk.

---

## Focus Skill: Theme

🔺 **Read the story. Then choose the best answer for each question.**

On Saturday afternoon, Mark was sad. He and his sister Beth had hoped to go to the movies. His mother had told him that they couldn't go unless their rooms were clean. Mark had put off cleaning all day even though his dad had warned him about using his time wisely. Now it was 3:20, and the movie would begin at 4:00. Looking at the big mess in his room Mark knew that there was no way he would be able to clean it fast enough.

Beth had started cleaning her room in the morning and was already done. Beth stopped by Mark's room to check on him. She could see right away that her help was needed.

"I'm going to help you out so that we can both go to the movies," Beth said. "You'd better start cleaning your room earlier next time, though." Mark agreed. It wasn't fair that Beth had to clean two rooms because he'd put off doing his own work. Working together, they cleaned Mark's room in record time.

"I think a treat is in order for all your hard work," Mark and Beth's mother said. "Let's get popcorn!"

1. What is Mark's problem?
   (A) Mark does not like going to the movies.
   (B) Mark put off cleaning his room.
   (C) Beth cleaned her room in the morning.
   (D) Beth was excited about the movie.

2. How does Mark solve his problem?
   (F) Beth helps him clean.
   (G) He starts cleaning early.
   (H) His mom gets him a treat.
   (I) He goes to the movies.

3. What do Beth's actions tell you about her?
   (A) She is helpful.
   (B) She is lazy.
   (C) She is funny.
   (D) She is curious.

4. What is the theme of the story?
   (F) Cleaning is hard work.
   (G) Going to the movies is fun.
   (H) It is best to use your time wisely.
   (I) Working together is difficult.

TOTAL SCORE: _____ /4

Name _____

## Follow Directions

▲ Read the passage. Then choose the best answer
for each question.

Learning new words can be fun. Also, having a larger
vocabulary will help you become a better reader. Read the steps
below to find out how to learn new words.

First, look for new words wherever you can find them. Read
books at school, and check out books from the library. Look
at magazines in the doctor's office, or read the cereal box at
breakfast. You'll soon see that exciting new words are all around
you.

Second, as you read, write down any new words that you find.
To keep all your new words in one place, you could make a new
words notebook. Decorate the cover with your favorite new
words.

Next, when you have a list of words, use a dictionary to find
out what they mean. Write the words and their definitions in
the notebook so that you can look at them later. Ask your parent
or teacher to help you use your new words in sentences.

Then be sure to reread the list in your notebook every day or
two. Studying the list will help you remember the new words.
Finally, have fun using your new words!

1. Which word lets you know that you are reading step one?
   Ⓐ Next
   Ⓑ Second
   Ⓒ First
   Ⓓ Finally

---

Name _____

2. What is step three?
   Ⓕ Look for new words.
   Ⓖ Use a dictionary.
   Ⓗ Make a list of words.
   Ⓘ Read the list in your notebook.

3. Which of these is a time-order word?
   Ⓐ look
   Ⓑ keep
   Ⓒ have
   Ⓓ second

4. Which word lets you know that you are reading the last
   step?
   Ⓕ Next
   Ⓖ Finally
   Ⓗ Then
   Ⓘ Second

TOTAL SCORE: _____ /4

# Robust Vocabulary

▲ **Choose the word that best completes each sentence.**

**1.** Maria felt _____ for the family that lost their home.

Ⓐ gratitude
Ⓑ memory
Ⓒ compassion
Ⓓ heritage

**2.** The _____ young man was always looking in the mirror.

Ⓕ vain
Ⓖ swift
Ⓗ enormous
Ⓘ dull

**3.** I _____ the sisters talking about the surprise party.

Ⓐ suggested
Ⓑ overheard
Ⓒ exclaimed
Ⓓ composed

**4.** Matt felt tired, so I _____ that he go to bed early.

Ⓕ composed
Ⓖ overheard
Ⓗ suggested
Ⓘ exclaimed

**5.** The elephant looked _____ next to the mouse.

Ⓐ dull
Ⓑ swift
Ⓒ vain
Ⓓ enormous

**6.** "Watch out!" she _____ loudly.

Ⓕ composed
Ⓖ yanked
Ⓗ exclaimed
Ⓘ overheard

**7.** I feel _____ toward the person who found my lost kitten.

Ⓐ compassion
Ⓑ gratitude
Ⓒ memory
Ⓓ masterpiece

**8.** The runner who was winning the race was _____.

Ⓕ swift
Ⓖ dull
Ⓗ vain
Ⓘ enormous

**9.** I _____ a short song for the talent show.

Ⓐ overheard
Ⓑ suggested
Ⓒ exclaimed
Ⓓ composed

**10.** Leslie _____ wrapped the small present in a large box.

Ⓕ gloriously
Ⓖ deliberately
Ⓗ heroically
Ⓘ vainly

TOTAL SCORE: _____ /10

## Grammar: Action Verbs

▲ Read each sentence. Choose the action verb in each sentence.

1. Everyone at the wedding danced for hours.
   - Ⓐ Everyone
   - Ⓑ wedding
   - Ⓒ danced
   - Ⓓ hours

2. The monkey ate a large banana.
   - Ⓕ monkey
   - Ⓖ ate
   - Ⓗ large
   - Ⓘ banana

3. Grandpa baked bread from his favorite recipe.
   - Ⓐ baked
   - Ⓑ bread
   - Ⓒ favorite
   - Ⓓ recipe

4. I hit my knee against the table.
   - Ⓕ hit
   - Ⓖ knee
   - Ⓗ against
   - Ⓘ table

TOTAL SCORE: _____ /4

---

## Oral Reading Fluency

You may think that dragons live only in fairy tales. | 10
Although there are no dragons that actually breathe fire | 19
or fly, there are lizards in the real world that are called | 31
Komodo dragons. | 33

Komodo dragons can grow to be ten feet long and | 43
can weigh up to 300 pounds. This makes them the | 53
heaviest lizards on Earth. They have scaly skin; long, flat | 63
heads; and strong, muscular tails. They have short legs | 72
but can still run up to eleven miles per hour for short | 84
periods of time. | 87

Komodo dragons are skilled hunters. They use their | 95
excellent sense of smell to help them find food. They also | 106
use camouflage to hide from their prey. They use their | 116
powerful jaws to eat deer, pigs, smaller dragons, and even | 126
water buffalo. | 128

Most Komodo dragons live in Indonesia. In America, | 136
one of the only places to find Komodo dragons is in | 147
zoos. Komodo dragons that live in zoos usually eat small | 157
animals such as mice and rabbits. The giant lizards can | 167
swallow these little animals whole. | 172

_____ /WCPM

Name _____

## Selection Comprehension

▲ **Choose the best answer for each question.**

1. What is the purpose of this interview?
   - Ⓐ to explain what the cast and crew of a play do
   - Ⓑ to get people to become play directors
   - Ⓒ to tell the story of *Sleeping Beauty*
   - Ⓓ to tell about a famous actor

2. How are all the jobs the SAME?
   - Ⓕ All act a part on a stage.
   - Ⓖ All run the soundboard.
   - Ⓗ All draw and sew costumes.
   - Ⓘ All need skill and hard work.

3. A designer would be MOST interested in
   - Ⓐ how an actor looks.
   - Ⓑ how an actor feels.
   - Ⓒ how an actor says lines.
   - Ⓓ how well an actor can be heard.

4. If the play's music is too loud, who is MOST LIKELY to fix the problem?
   - Ⓕ the actor
   - Ⓖ the crew leader
   - Ⓗ the designer
   - Ⓘ the director

Name _____

5. Which sentence is an OPINION from the play?
   - Ⓐ First, I chose the script.
   - Ⓑ The play will open tonight to a sold-out crowd.
   - Ⓒ That sounds like fun!
   - Ⓓ I went to an art school.

6. About how long did it take to get *Sleeping Beauty* ready for opening night?
   - Ⓕ one day
   - Ⓖ two days
   - Ⓗ two months
   - Ⓘ six months

7. Who helps actors decide how to say their lines?
   - Ⓐ the crew leader
   - Ⓑ the designer
   - Ⓒ the director
   - Ⓓ the other actors

8. Which idea BEST shows that putting on a play is hard work?
   - Ⓕ The director has to give tips.
   - Ⓖ The designer works with a team.
   - Ⓗ The designer reads about famous artists.
   - Ⓘ The cast and crew have to practice many days.

## Robust Vocabulary

▲ Choose the word that best completes each sentence.

1. The end of the story made me sad because it was _____.
   - (A) mandatory
   - (B) flawless
   - (C) tragic
   - (D) limp

2. They spent time together and enjoyed a sense of _____.
   - (F) camaraderie
   - (G) masterpiece
   - (H) dialogue
   - (I) gratitude

3. The dancers wanted to _____ more before opening night.
   - (A) immerse
   - (B) suggest
   - (C) criticize
   - (D) rehearse

4. The diamond is very valuable because it is _____.
   - (F) mandatory
   - (G) tragic
   - (H) flawless
   - (I) limp

5. You must _____ yourself in water to swim.
   - (A) immerse
   - (B) rehearse
   - (C) criticize
   - (D) suggest

Robust Vocabulary

© Harcourt • Grade 3

213

Name _____

READ
THINK
EXPLAIN

Weekly
Lesson Test
Lesson 20

## Written Response (worth two points)

9. Which job is the hardest to do when putting on a play? Explain why that job is the hardest. Use information and details from "Backstage with Chris and Casey" to support your answer.

Sample two-point response: The director has the hardest

job. The director is in charge of the whole show.

_____

_____

TOTAL SCORE: _____ /8 + _____ /2

Selection Comprehension
"Backstage with Chris and Casey"
© Harcourt • Grade 3

212

## Selection Comprehension

▲ Choose the best answer for each question.

**1.** How can readers tell that "Antarctic Ice" is nonfiction?
- (A) It has a plot that teaches a lesson.
- (B) It tells about real places and animals.
- (C) It tells the author's personal feelings.
- (D) It has events that could never happen.

**2.** Based on the article, Antarctica is special because it has
- (F) the coldest weather in the world.
- (G) the most animals in the world.
- (H) the strongest winds on earth.
- (I) the shortest winters on earth.

**3.** What is unusual about Antarctica in the summer?
- (A) Animals are busy.
- (B) There is no night time.
- (C) Some ice starts to melt.
- (D) The sun rises in the sky.

**4.** What is one way that seals, penguins, and fish in Antarctica are ALIKE?
- (F) All are helped in some way by the ice.
- (G) All breathe through cracks in the ice.
- (H) All grow very fast in winter.
- (I) All lay only one or two eggs.

---

**6.** I had a hard time hearing the _____ between the two characters in the play because one spoke softly.
- (F) masterpiece
- (G) gratitude
- (H) camaraderie
- (I) dialogue

**7.** She said it was _____ for everyone to attend the assembly.
- (A) tragic
- (B) mandatory
- (C) flawless
- (D) limp

**8.** After running my first long race, my legs felt _____.
- (F) limp
- (G) mandatory
- (H) tragic
- (I) flawless

**9.** I will not _____ her because she did a great job.
- (A) rehearse
- (B) suggest
- (C) immerse
- (D) criticize

**10.** There are two _____ of my favorite fairy tale.
- (F) compassions
- (G) versions
- (H) burdens
- (I) camaraderie

**Robust Vocabulary**

TOTAL SCORE: _____ /10

READ
THINK
EXPLAIN

## Written Response (worth two points)

9. **COMPARING TEXTS** Describe what you would expect to see if you went to Antarctica. Use information from BOTH "Antarctic Ice" AND "Diary of a Very Short Winter Day" to support your answer.

**Sample two-point response: I would expect to see**

penguins, seals, fish, and whales. Everything would be

covered with ice. Fish would hide in the ice. Penguins

would lay eggs and stand on the ice. The parent penguins

would go in the ocean to get food to bring back to the

chicks.

_____

TOTAL SCORE: _____ /8 + _____ /2

---

5. What happens when there is no sunshine in Antarctica?

　Ⓐ Seal pups cannot grow thick fur.

　Ⓑ Underwater animals cannot move.

　Ⓒ Fish cannot hide in holes in the ice.

　Ⓓ Plants cannot grow.

6. What happens JUST AFTER summer ends in Antarctica?

　Ⓕ Male penguins sit on eggs to keep them warm.

　Ⓖ Penguin parents bring food to their chicks.

　Ⓗ Penguin chicks swim north for the winter.

　Ⓘ Male penguins build nests out of stones.

7. What causes ice algae to move to the bottom of the sea?

　Ⓐ The algae go to the bottom to hide from seals.

　Ⓑ The wind blows the algae to the ocean floor.

　Ⓒ The algae go lower to escape from the sun.

　Ⓓ The ice that the algae live on melts.

8. What can readers tell about the author of this article?

　Ⓕ The author has always lived in Antarctica.

　Ⓖ The author likes winter more than summer.

　Ⓗ The author knows a lot about science and wildlife.

　Ⓘ The author thinks everyone should travel to Antarctica.

## Phonics/Spelling: Vowel Variants

### /o͞o/oo, ew, ue, ui; /o͝o/oo

▲ **Read the sentence. Choose the word from the sentence that has the same vowel sound as _moon_ or _foot_.**

1. The ripe fruit in the basket is sweet.

   Ⓐ ripe
   **Ⓑ fruit**
   Ⓒ basket
   Ⓓ sweet

2. A bird flew over the rosebush.

   **Ⓕ flew**
   Ⓖ bird
   Ⓗ the
   Ⓘ over

3. We will fix the broken doll with glue.

   Ⓐ fix
   **Ⓑ glue**
   Ⓒ doll
   Ⓓ broken

4. He wanted the book with the red cover.

   Ⓕ wanted
   Ⓖ red
   **Ⓗ book**
   Ⓘ cover

Phonics/Spelling: Vowel Variants
/o͞o/oo, ew, ue, ui; /o͝o/oo
© Harcourt • Grade 3

---

## Focus Skill: Sequence

▲ **Read the passage. Then choose the best answer for each question.**

On Sunday afternoon, Bruce and Libby wanted to fly kites at the park. Unfortunately, they did not have kites. Bruce and Libby decided to make their own kites.

First, they asked their older brother, Philip, to help them. Next, they gathered the supplies they would need. In the kitchen, Philip found straws to make the frame for the kites. Libby looked through her art supplies and found brightly colored paper to use. Bruce searched the garage and found strong string.

Then, Bruce and Libby used the colored paper to make designs for their kites while Philip taped the straws into two diamond-shaped frames. Libby made her kite look like a rainbow. Bruce designed his kite to look like a shooting star. Philip helped Bruce and Libby glue their kites to the frames and tie string to the bottom.

Finally, Bruce, Libby, and Philip walked to the park. They couldn't wait to watch their new kites fly!

1. Which event happens first?

   **Ⓐ Bruce and Libby want to fly kites.**
   Ⓑ Bruce and Libby tie string to their kites.
   Ⓒ Bruce and Libby make colorful designs.
   Ⓓ Bruce and Libby use colored paper.

Focus Skill: Sequence
© Harcourt • Grade 3

TOTAL SCORE: _____ /4

Name _____

## Author's Message

▲ Read the passage. Then choose the best answer for each question.

The Sahara in North Africa is the largest desert in the world. Deserts are areas of Earth that receive very little rain and have high daytime temperatures. Life in the desert is difficult. Animals that live in the Sahara have found ways to survive the harsh conditions.

The fennec fox escapes the desert heat by living in tunnels in the sand during the day. The fox comes out when it is cooler at night to hunt for food.

The addax is a large animal. It lives well in the desert because it does not have to drink water often. Instead, the addax gets water from the desert grasses and bushes it eats every day.

These animals, and others such as camels, sheep, and many types of birds, have found ways to make the desert their home.

1. What does the author say about the Sahara?
   - Ⓐ It is in North America.
   - **Ⓑ It is the largest desert on Earth.**
   - Ⓒ It receives plenty of rain.
   - Ⓓ It is cool during the day.

2. Why did the author include facts about the fennec fox and addax?
   - **Ⓕ to explain how two desert animals survive**
   - Ⓖ to tell a story about two interesting animals
   - Ⓗ to describe how desert animals play games
   - Ⓘ to show how to take care of desert animals

Author's Message
© Harcourt • Grade 3
221

---

Name _____

2. What happens after Bruce and Libby ask Philip to help them?
   - Ⓕ They walk to the park.
   - **Ⓖ They gather the supplies.**
   - Ⓗ They decide to make kites.
   - Ⓘ They glue their kites to the frames.

3. Which event happens last?
   - Ⓐ Bruce and Libby make colorful designs.
   - Ⓑ Philip makes kite frames with straws.
   - Ⓒ Bruce finds strong string in the garage.
   - **Ⓓ Bruce, Libby, and Philip walk to the park.**

4. Which is a time-order word?
   - **Ⓕ finally**
   - Ⓖ used
   - Ⓗ wait
   - Ⓘ watch

Focus Skill: Sequence
© Harcourt • Grade 3
220

TOTAL SCORE: _____ /4

## Robust Vocabulary

▲ **Choose the word that best completes each sentence.**

1. The gray, _____ weather made me feel sleepy.
   - Ⓐ bleak
   - Ⓑ dim
   - Ⓒ scarce
   - Ⓓ strict

2. Some jewels are more valuable because they are _____.
   - Ⓕ strict
   - Ⓖ harsh
   - Ⓗ dim
   - Ⓘ scarce

3. My friend's _____ words hurt my feelings.
   - Ⓐ strict
   - Ⓑ bleak
   - Ⓒ dim
   - Ⓓ harsh

4. Enrique lazily _____ down the river on his raft.
   - Ⓕ drifts
   - Ⓖ suggests
   - Ⓗ criticizes
   - Ⓘ shelters

5. I could not read because the lights were too _____.
   - Ⓐ harsh
   - Ⓑ dim
   - Ⓒ bleak
   - Ⓓ strict

**Robust Vocabulary**

© Harcourt • Grade 3

223

---

3. What might the author's message be?
   - Ⓐ Traveling in the Sahara is difficult.
   - Ⓑ Water is hard to find in the Sahara.
   - Ⓒ Animals in the Sahara survive the harsh conditions.
   - Ⓓ Most animals leave the Sahara because of the heat.

4. What did you learn from this selection?
   - Ⓕ Fennec foxes spend the day in tunnels.
   - Ⓖ Camels get water from the plants they eat.
   - Ⓗ The addax is a small, desert animal.
   - Ⓘ Many birds search for food at night.

**Author's Message**

© Harcourt • Grade 3

222

**TOTAL SCORE:** _____ /4

---

Name _____

# Grammar: The Verb Be

▲ Choose the word that correctly completes each sentence.

1. The chickens _____ eating in the yard.
   - Ⓐ is
   - Ⓑ was
   - Ⓒ were
   - Ⓓ am

2. Do you think Sonya _____ coming?
   - Ⓕ are
   - Ⓖ is
   - Ⓗ were
   - Ⓘ am

3. I _____ happy to see you.
   - Ⓐ am
   - Ⓑ is
   - Ⓒ are
   - Ⓓ were

4. The dogs _____ running down the hill.
   - Ⓕ were
   - Ⓖ was
   - Ⓗ am
   - Ⓘ is

Grammar: The Verb Be

TOTAL SCORE: _____ /4

© Harcourt • Grade 3

---

Name _____

6. Joan was unsure whether she would leave the sofa there _____, but she left it for now.
   - Ⓕ permanently
   - Ⓖ deliberately
   - Ⓗ harshly
   - Ⓘ swiftly

7. To help our planet, natural resources need to be _____.
   - Ⓐ rehearsed
   - Ⓑ conserved
   - Ⓒ criticized
   - Ⓓ absence

8. The _____ rules seemed unfair to the members of the team.
   - Ⓕ strict
   - Ⓖ dim
   - Ⓗ bleak
   - Ⓘ scarce

9. What _____ people waiting for the bus from the rain?
   - Ⓐ criticizes
   - Ⓑ suggests
   - Ⓒ shelters
   - Ⓓ drifts

10. When Zhang missed school, his mother called to explain his _____.
    - Ⓕ conserved
    - Ⓖ version
    - Ⓗ camaraderie
    - Ⓘ absence

Robust Vocabulary

TOTAL SCORE: _____ /10

© Harcourt • Grade 3

---

*Student Edition* pp. 224–225

© Harcourt • Grade 3

## Oral Reading Fluency

I've always known I wanted to be a dog detective. I   11
was strolling through the park one day, when WHAM!   20
I was knocked over by an enormous black dog.   29

"Hey!" I shouted, but the dog didn't stop. I looked   39
around for the dog's owner. When I didn't see anyone, I   50
took off after the dog. He raced down the path toward   61
the lake. I was running so fast after him that I slipped and   74
landed right in a mud puddle.   80

"He'll get away," I thought as I tried to wipe the mud   92
from my eyes.   95

I wasn't having much luck when, suddenly, I felt   104
something warm licking my face. The dog had come   113
back, and he was helping me.   119

His rough tongue tickled my nose and I started   128
laughing, even though my clothes were covered in mud.   137
I checked the dog's tags and realized that he was Mrs.   148
Davidson's dog Lucky, who had been missing for over a   158
week. When she heard that I "captured" Lucky, she said   168
I was the best dog detective in the world!   177

_____ /WCPM

---

## Selection Comprehension

▲ **Choose the best answer for each question.**

**1.** Why did the author write "Bat Loves the Night"?

  Ⓐ to persuade readers to get a bat

  ● Ⓑ to teach interesting facts about bats

  Ⓒ to compare two different kinds of bats

  Ⓓ to warn readers why bats are dangerous

**2.** Based on the article, what do bats MOSTLY use to find their way?

  ● Ⓕ sound

  Ⓖ touch

  Ⓗ smell

  Ⓘ sight

**3.** What is unusual about the way bats sleep?

  Ⓐ They sleep with their eyes open.

  Ⓑ They need very little sleep.

  Ⓒ They sleep while they fly.

  ● Ⓓ They sleep upside down.

**4.** How old are bats when they learn to fly?

  Ⓕ one day old

  Ⓖ one week old

  ● Ⓗ a few weeks old

  Ⓘ several months old

5. Where is a bat MOST LIKELY to be found during the day?

(A) smelling flowers in a garden

(B) chasing flies in a yard

(C) sleeping in a cave

(D) hiding in a hedge

6. Why does the author compare a bat's feet to a coat hanger?

(F) because both weigh very little

(G) because both have a dark color

(H) because both are made of wire

(I) because both have a curved hook

7. Based on the article, which is a bat MOST LIKELY to eat?

(A) an owl

(B) a hawk

(C) a spider

(D) a snake

8. How can readers tell that "Bat Loves the Night" is nonfiction?

(F) It gives facts and information about a subject.

(G) It tells true events that happened long ago.

(H) It tells a story and has rhyming words.

(I) It explains why a person is important.

## Written Response (worth two points)

READ
THINK
EXPLAIN

9. Explain why "Bat Loves the Night" is a good title for this article. Use information and details from the article to help you explain.

**Sample two-point response: Bats sleep during the day but come out at night. That is when they leave the roost to hunt for their food.**

_____

_____

TOTAL SCORE: _____ /8 + _____ /2

Name _____

## Focus Skill: Sequence

▲ Read the passage. Then choose the best answer for each question.

### Time to Wake Up

When Jamal woke up this morning, he did not want to get out of bed. He had been reading the previous night. He enjoyed reading before going to sleep.

It was raining, and Jamal liked listening to the pitter-patter of raindrops on the window.

Then, Jamal's dad called, "It's time for breakfast! Hurry up or you'll be late for the school bus."

Jamal jumped up and put on his clothes before he rushed downstairs to the kitchen.

"Well, glad you finally decided to get up, son," joked his dad. Jamal ate a quick breakfast. Then he grabbed his backpack and gave his dad a quick hug.

Jamal dashed out the door. Finally, he made it to the corner just as the bus arrived.

1. What does Jamal do first?
   Ⓐ He wakes up.
   Ⓑ He eats breakfast.
   Ⓒ He listens to the rain.
   Ⓓ He catches the bus.

Focus Skill: Sequence
© Harcourt • Grade 3

---

Name _____

## Phonics/Spelling: Vowel Variant /ô/, au(gh), ough, aw, a(l), o

▲ Read each model word. Then fill in the circle next to the word that has the same sound as the underlined part of the model word and completes each sentence.

1. **false**
   When I'm tired I _____.
   Ⓐ sleep
   Ⓑ yawn
   Ⓒ read
   Ⓓ laugh

2. **lost**
   You _____ to close the window when it rains.
   Ⓕ ought
   Ⓖ need
   Ⓗ should
   Ⓘ help

3. **pause**
   I like to _____ in the park.
   Ⓐ cough
   Ⓑ play
   Ⓒ walk
   Ⓓ sit

4. **caught**
   We were _____ late to catch the bus.
   Ⓕ nearly
   Ⓖ taught
   Ⓗ almost
   Ⓘ hardly

TOTAL SCORE: _____ /4

Phonics/Spelling: Vowel Variant /ô/, au (gh), ough, aw, a(l), o
© Harcourt • Grade 3

---

***Student Edition** pp. 230–231*

© Harcourt • Grade 3

## Author's Message

▲ Read the passage. Then choose the best answer for each question.

Rain forests are important to Earth. Most rain forests are found close to the equator. Rain forests are important because many animals, plants, and insects live in the shaded, hot, damp forests. More animals, plants, and insects live in rain forests than almost anywhere else on Earth.

The animals, insects, and plants of the rain forest depend on each other. Many trees depend on animals to help spread their seeds. Some trees depend on insects, such as stinging ants, which live in them to defend the tree from plant-eating animals. The ants sting any hungry animals that climb their trees.

Animals depend on trees and plants to provide them with food and places to live. Trees can also provide animals safety. Monkeys swing and glide between trees using their special tails to help them. Flying squirrels leap from tree to tree. Staying high up in the branches to live, eat, and play protects these animals from other animals, such as bears and leopards, on the forest floor.

1. What does the author say about rain forests?
   - (A) Rain forests are found close to the equator.
   - (B) Rain forests are cool and dry.
   - (C) Rain forests are unimportant to Earth.
   - (D) Rain forests are homes to a few types of animals.

---

2. What does Jamal do after his dad calls him to breakfast?
   - (F) Jamal dashes out the door to catch the bus.
   - (G) Jamal jumps up and gets dressed.
   - (H) Jamal gives his dad a hug.
   - (I) Jamal falls back to sleep.

3. What happens as Jamal reaches the corner?
   - (A) His dad calls to him.
   - (B) The bus arrives.
   - (C) Jamal leaves the house.
   - (D) Jamal falls back to sleep.

4. Which is a time-order word?
   - (F) on
   - (G) for
   - (H) then
   - (I) under

TOTAL SCORE: _____ /4

## Robust Vocabulary

▲ Choose the word that best completes each sentence.

1. The flowers were _____ with snow.
   - Ⓐ conserved
   - Ⓑ blanketed
   - Ⓒ inverted
   - Ⓓ criticized

2. Our _____ on the mountain were beautiful.
   - Ⓕ dialogues
   - Ⓖ surroundings
   - Ⓗ plummet
   - Ⓘ absences

3. My mother asked me to make an _____ to do my chores.
   - Ⓐ inverted
   - Ⓑ absence
   - Ⓒ under
   - Ⓓ effort

4. The bird _____ down from the sky to catch a mouse.
   - Ⓕ drifts
   - Ⓖ dozes
   - Ⓗ swoops
   - Ⓘ shelters

5. I forgot an important _____ I needed to tell my mother.
   - Ⓐ detail
   - Ⓑ effort
   - Ⓒ absence
   - Ⓓ inverted

Robust Vocabulary

---

2. Why did the author include facts about stinging ants?
   - Ⓕ to show how insects and plants depend on each other
   - Ⓖ to explain how trees grow in the forest
   - Ⓗ to describe how insects find food on the forest floor
   - Ⓘ to tell how to find different types of plants in the forest

3. What might the author's message be?
   - Ⓐ Animals help spread seeds.
   - Ⓑ Rain forests are important.
   - Ⓒ The climate at the equator is warm.
   - Ⓓ Many insects live in rain forests.

4. What did you learn from the selection?
   - Ⓕ Bears depend on trees for places to live in the forest.
   - Ⓖ Flying squirrels search for food on the forest floor.
   - Ⓗ Stinging ants live under the ground.
   - Ⓘ Monkeys use their tails to swing between trees.

TOTAL SCORE: _____ /4

Author's Message

## Grammar: Main and Helping Verbs

▲ Choose the best answer for each question.

**1.** What is the helping verb in this sentence?

   **Rachel is working hard today.**

   Ⓐ working
   Ⓑ today
   Ⓒ is
   Ⓓ hard

**2.** What is the helping verb in this sentence?

   **We were running fast at recess.**

   Ⓕ were
   Ⓖ running
   Ⓗ recess
   Ⓘ fast

**3.** What is the main verb in this sentence?

   **We have hidden the marble behind the books.**

   Ⓐ hidden
   Ⓑ behind
   Ⓒ books
   Ⓓ have

**4.** What is the main verb in this sentence?

   **The bird is sitting on my windowsill.**

   Ⓕ is
   Ⓖ sitting
   Ⓗ bird
   Ⓘ windowsill

Grammar: Main and Helping Verbs

© Harcourt • Grade 3

TOTAL SCORE: _____ /4

237

---

**6.** I heard the flag _____ outside the window.

   Ⓕ nocturnal
   Ⓖ fluttering
   Ⓗ harsh
   Ⓘ dim

**7.** The _____ animals in the forest come out at night.

   Ⓐ fluttering
   Ⓑ dim
   Ⓒ nocturnal
   Ⓓ bleak

**8.** Sally _____ in a big chair by the window.

   Ⓕ drifts
   Ⓖ shelters
   Ⓗ swoops
   Ⓘ dozes

**9.** When the wind stopped blowing, my kite began to _____.

   Ⓐ plummet
   Ⓑ shelter
   Ⓒ blanket
   Ⓓ rehearse

**10.** The _____ sign in the window was difficult to read.

   Ⓕ harsh
   Ⓖ dim
   Ⓗ plummet
   Ⓘ scarce

**Robust Vocabulary**

© Harcourt • Grade 3

TOTAL SCORE: _____ /10

236

---

***Student Edition*** *pp. 236–237*

149

© Harcourt • Grade 3

## Selection Comprehension

▲ Choose the best answer for each question.

**1.** How can readers tell that "Chestnut Cove" is a fantasy?

Ⓐ The main character is a famous person.

Ⓑ The story has acts that are divided into scenes.

Ⓒ The characters and events are not like real life.

Ⓓ The story tells true events that happened in the past.

**2.** What happened RIGHT AFTER King Milford made his announcement about growing the largest watermelon?

Ⓕ The villagers saw a family have a somersault race.

Ⓖ People laughed and went on with their day.

Ⓗ The shopkeepers opened their doors.

Ⓘ All the children left for school.

**3.** Why did the villagers decide to grow watermelons?

Ⓐ They wanted to please the king.

Ⓑ They liked being in an exciting contest.

Ⓒ They knew it would be fun to do together.

Ⓓ They started thinking of things they wanted.

**4.** How do the villagers change in the story?

Ⓕ At first they are busy, but then they get lazy.

Ⓖ At first they are happy, but then they get greedy.

Ⓗ At first they are careful, but then they get careless.

Ⓘ At first they are frightened, but then they get brave.

---

## Oral Reading Fluency

Deserts are places on Earth that are very hot and dry. It 12

is difficult for most animals to survive in deserts. However, 22

some animals, such as camels, are made to live in deserts. 33

Camels can survive in the desert because they go 42

for long periods of time without drinking water. This is 52

helpful in the dry, dusty desert where water is hard to 63

find. When camels find water, they drink plenty of it. After 74

filling up, camels can go a week or more and not drink 86

another drop. 88

Camels have either one hump or two humps on their 98

backs. Some people think camels store water in their 107

humps, but camels really store food in their humps. 116

Because their bodies store food, camels can go months 125

between meals. This helps them survive in the desert 134

when they cannot find food for a long period of time. 145

Camels also do not seem to mind the hot weather 155

and desert sandstorms. They can withstand very high 163

temperatures without sweating. They have two rows 170

of long eyelashes to protect their eyes from desert 179

sandstorms. 180

/WCPM _____

5. What is the villagers' BIGGEST problem in the story?

Ⓐ They think their king is not fair.

Ⓑ They start having to get up early.

Ⓒ They stop trying to help each other.

Ⓓ They cannot get their plants to grow.

6. Which action BEST shows that the villagers were different after the king's contest was announced?

Ⓕ They turned the soil.

Ⓖ They stayed busy in their gardens.

Ⓗ They worked late in the afternoon.

Ⓘ They fought over whose watermelon was best.

7. Which event brings all the villagers together as friends?

Ⓐ Joe Morgan saves Mrs. Lark's pig.

Ⓑ Mrs. Lark sleeps in her garden one night.

Ⓒ Mrs. Phillips's goat gets stuck in a bench.

Ⓓ Joe Morgan grew a big watermelon.

8. Which lesson can be learned from this story?

Ⓕ Friends are more important than riches.

Ⓖ To do a job right, do it yourself.

Ⓗ Harsh words cannot be taken back.

Ⓘ It is always best to plan ahead.

---

READ
THINK
EXPLAIN

## Written Response (worth two points)

9. How can you tell that the events in "Chestnut Cove" could not really happen? Use information and details from the story to help you explain.

**Sample two-point response: A fish would not drink up all the water in a pond. It would be hard for a cow to get stuck in a tree. A king would not trade his kingdom for a watermelon.**

TOTAL SCORE: _____ /8 + _____ /2

## Phonics/Spelling: Prefixes *pre-, mis-, in-*

▲ Choose the word that correctly completes each sentence.

1. You should not _____ someone by telling a lie.

   Ⓐ inlead
   Ⓑ prelead
   Ⓒ mislead
   Ⓓ lead

2. Billy's teacher was unhappy because his homework was _____.

   Ⓕ complete
   Ⓖ incomplete
   Ⓗ completely
   Ⓘ completed

3. Before you bake a cake, you must _____ the oven.

   Ⓐ preheat
   Ⓑ heat
   Ⓒ heats
   Ⓓ unheat

4. Sarah lost points on her test when she wrote the _____ answer.

   Ⓕ correct
   Ⓖ incorrect
   Ⓗ correctly
   Ⓘ correcting

Phonics/Spelling: Prefixes *pre-, mis-, in-*    242

© Harcourt • Grade 3

---

## Focus Skill: Cause and Effect

▲ Read the passage. Then choose the best answer for each question.

Jessie wanted to do something special for her sister, Leah. Leah had a cold and didn't feel well. She hadn't been able to play outside all day. Jessie knew that her sister was bored resting in bed while Jessie and their brother Sam played together.

Jessie asked her mother for ideas. Her mother suggested that Jessie and Sam perform a skit for Leah. Jessie thought that sounded like fun. She knew that Leah would like it, too.

Jessie asked Sam to help her. She and Sam put on silly costumes and then practiced their skit several times for their mother.

When Jessie and Sam entered Leah's room, she began laughing as soon as she saw the silly costumes they were wearing.

"We've made up a skit for you because you couldn't play with us today," Jessie said.

After the skit, Leah clapped loudly. "That was a wonderful surprise," she said. "Thanks to you, I feel better already."

1. Why does Jessie want to do something special for Leah?

   Ⓐ Leah does not feel well.
   Ⓑ Jessie forgot Leah's birthday.
   Ⓒ Leah is upset with her.
   Ⓓ Jessie does not want to play outside.

Focus Skill: Cause and Effect    243

© Harcourt • Grade 3

TOTAL SCORE: _____ /4

---

Name _____

2. What happens when Jessie asks Sam to help her?
  F They put on silly costumes.
  G They make lunch for Leah.
  H They go outside to play.
  I They draw pictures for Leah.

3. What happens when Leah sees Jessie and Sam in their costumes?
  A Leah asks their mother to take a picture.
  B Leah tells them that they look silly.
  C Leah is sad that she cannot play.
  D Leah begins to laugh.

4. Why does Leah thank Jessie and Sam?
  F They asked her to play with them.
  G They took her soup.
  H They helped her feel better.
  I They bought her a special present.

Focus Skill: Cause and Effect

© Harcourt • Grade 3

244

---

Name _____

# Homophones

▲ Choose the best answer for each question.

1. Read this sentence.

   The boat moved quickly over the water after we lifted the sail.

   What is the meaning of the word *sail* in this sentence?
   A a large piece of material used to catch the wind
   B a period of time when stores sell goods at lower prices
   C to move smoothly and quickly
   D to leave in a boat or a ship

2. Read this sentence.

   We need four more pencils.

   What is the meaning of the word *four* in this sentence?
   F to be received
   G a number
   H the front of something
   I to be helped

3. Read this sentence.

   My favorite hare was soft, white, and fluffy.

   What is the meaning of the word *hare* in this sentence?
   A what grows on your head
   B a tall, thin plant
   C a large rabbit
   D a tiny amount

TOTAL SCORE: ____ /4

Homophones

© Harcourt • Grade 3

245

---

## Robust Vocabulary

▲ **Choose the word that best completes each sentence.**

1. What kind of _____ are you feeling now?

    (A) fondness

    (B) emotion

    (C) detail

    (D) surroundings

2. My mother has a _____ for spending time in the park.

    (F) decent

    (G) fondness

    (H) plummet

    (I) detail

3. Do you think Judy looked _____ in her costume?

    (A) ridiculous

    (B) detail

    (C) bleak

    (D) strict

4. John _____ his school supplies to another desk.

    (F) contented

    (G) transferred

    (H) blanketed

    (I) inverted

5. The children _____ waited for the dessert.

    (A) harshly

    (B) eagerly

    (C) disgraceful

    (D) strictly

Robust Vocabulary

© Harcourt • Grade 3

247

4. Read this sentence.

    **Let's meet right after class today in the hallway.**

    What is the meaning of the word *meet* in this sentence?

    (F) to get together

    (G) the flesh of animals

    (H) a swimming contest

    (I) to be introduced

5. Read this sentence.

    **I know all fifty states and capitals.**

    What is the meaning of the word *know* in this sentence?

    (A) to disagree with

    (B) to recognize someone

    (C) to see differences

    (D) to have information

Homophones

© Harcourt • Grade 3

246

TOTAL SCORE: _____ /5

Name _____

# Grammar: Present-Tense Verbs

▲ Choose the word or words that correctly complete each sentence.

**1.** My cat _____ in the sun.
- Ⓐ is sleep
- Ⓑ was sleep
- Ⓒ sleeps
- Ⓓ sleeping

**2.** The dog _____ after the fox.
- Ⓕ is runs
- Ⓖ running
- Ⓗ runs
- Ⓘ will running

**3.** You should _____ with me after school.
- Ⓐ swam
- Ⓑ swims
- Ⓒ swim
- Ⓓ swimming

**4.** My little brother _____ quickly.
- Ⓕ is growing
- Ⓖ am growing
- Ⓗ are growing
- Ⓘ will growing

Grammar: Present-Tense Verbs

© Harcourt • Grade 3

TOTAL SCORE: _____ /4

---

Name _____

**6.** Everyone felt _____ after eating the big meal.
- Ⓕ contented
- Ⓖ disgraceful
- Ⓗ ridiculous
- Ⓘ bleak

**7.** I hope to _____ my grandmother's ring.
- Ⓐ transfer
- Ⓑ collaborate
- Ⓒ plummet
- Ⓓ inherit

**8.** My father said that my messy room was in _____ shape.
- Ⓕ disgraceful
- Ⓖ strict
- Ⓗ contented
- Ⓘ decent

**9.** Let's _____ on this project so we can finish more quickly.
- Ⓐ swoop
- Ⓑ doze
- Ⓒ collaborate
- Ⓓ inherit

**10.** Though I'm not the best at soccer, I am a _____ player.
- Ⓕ disgraceful
- Ⓖ swoop
- Ⓗ decent
- Ⓘ ridiculous

Robust Vocabulary

© Harcourt • Grade 3

TOTAL SCORE: _____ /10

---

***Student Edition** pp. 248–249*

© Harcourt • Grade 3

Name _____

## Oral Reading Fluency

President Abraham Lincoln's youngest son was named                    7

Thomas. Lincoln gave him the nickname "tadpole" when              15

his son was born because the president thought Thomas           24

looked like a tadpole. Most people called the boy Tad.              34

Tad was very close to his father.                                                       41

One year when Tad was ten, a turkey was sent to the            53

White House for the Lincoln family dinner during the            62

holidays. Tad named the turkey "Jack." He taught Jack to       72

follow him around the White House. When Tad found out       82

that the turkey was to be cooked for dinner, he was very        94

upset.                                                                                                     95

President Lincoln was in the middle of an important           104

meeting. Tad burst into the room, crying. He begged his         114

father to spare Jack's life. Lincoln thought carefully about     123

what to do. Then he took out a sheet of paper and wrote      136

an order. He wrote that Jack's life would be saved.                   146

Since that day, the President spares a turkey's life                155

before every Thanksgiving Day. This is part of a long            165

tradition that began with Abraham Lincoln's son Tad.           173

Oral Reading Fluency

© Harcourt • Grade 3

250

_____ /WCPM

---

Name _____

## Selection Comprehension

▲ Choose the best answer for each question.

1. How can readers tell that "Ramona Quimby, Age 8" is
   realistic fiction?

   (A) It explains how a place came to be.

   (B) It has animals that act like people.

   (C) It has events that could never happen in real life.

   **(D)** It has characters with feelings that real people have.

2. What is Ramona's problem in the story?

   (F) She left the book for her report at school.

   (G) She cannot get anyone to read her book report.

   **(H)** She wants to give a book report that is special.

   (I) She wants to give a report on a different book.

3. At first, why does Ramona have trouble thinking of a way
   to sell her book to anyone?

   (A) She has not read the whole book yet.

   (B) She thinks the book is too hard to read.

   (C) She does not really like the book herself.

   (D) She does not understand the book ending.

4. Where does Ramona get the idea for her report?

   **(F)** from watching television

   (G) from her friends, Sara and Janet

   (H) from something Danny said to her

   (I) from listening to other classmates

Selection Comprehension
"Ramona Quimby, Age 8"
© Harcourt • Grade 3

251

Name _____

5. What is the MAIN reason Ramona raises her hand to give her report before lunch?
- (A) She feels proud of her report idea.
- (B) She wants to get the report over with.
- (C) She wants Mrs. Whaley to like her.
- (D) She will get a better grade for speaking early.

6. When compared with the reports her classmates gave, Ramona's report
- (F) lasts much longer.
- (G) is more unusual.
- (H) is just the same.
- (I) has more facts.

7. Why do Ramona's face and ears turn red at the end of her report?
- (A) She feels angry.
- (B) She has a high fever.
- (C) She feels embarrassed.
- (D) She is getting sick again.

8. What can readers tell about Ramona?
- (F) She has given many reports.
- (G) She has a good imagination.
- (H) She reads books only about cats.
- (I) She never worries about anything.

**Selection Comprehension**
"Ramona Quimby, Age 8"
© Harcourt • Grade 3

---

Name _____

READ
THINK
EXPLAIN

## Written Response (worth two points)

9. Would you like to have Ramona as a friend? Use information and details from "Ramona Quimby, Age 8" to help you explain why or why not.

Sample two-point response: Yes, I would like to be friends with Ramona. She cares what people think of her. She is smart and funny. She has good ideas.

_____

TOTAL SCORE: _____ /8 + _____ /2

**Selection Comprehension**
"Ramona Quimby, Age 8"
© Harcourt • Grade 3

---

*Student Edition* pp. 252–253

157

© Harcourt • Grade 3

## Phonics/Spelling: Schwa /ə/

▲ Read each model word. Then fill in the circle next to the word that has the same sound as the underlined part of the model word and completes each sentence.

**1. above**

The movie was so good that I want to see it _____.

- Ⓐ more
- ● Ⓑ again
- Ⓒ now
- Ⓓ later

**2. applause**

Our teacher asked us to put a _____ on our new books.

- ● Ⓕ cover
- Ⓖ lid
- Ⓗ wrap
- Ⓘ sheet

**3. ever**

I was _____ when she called early in the morning.

- ● Ⓐ tired
- Ⓑ awake
- Ⓒ ready
- Ⓓ eating

**4. agree**

I left my bag _____ the table.

- Ⓕ by
- Ⓖ on
- Ⓗ near
- ● Ⓘ upon

---

## Focus Skill: Cause and Effect

▲ Read the passage. Then choose the best answer for each question.

### Packing for Camp

Ben was going on a camping trip, and he had to decide what to pack. The weather report said that it might rain, so Ben packed a raincoat and hat with his clothes. He also packed sunscreen and extra socks. He didn't want his toes to get cold at night.

When Ben finished packing, his backpack was too full and he'd forgotten one of the most important things—his flashlight. Ben took out his baseball and baseball glove so that he would have room for his flashlight. He kept his flashlight because he knew it would come in handy at night.

**1.** Why does Ben pack a raincoat and hat?

- Ⓐ His mother tells him to pack them.
- Ⓑ He always prepares for every kind of weather.
- ● Ⓒ The weather report says that it might rain.
- Ⓓ He enjoys playing in puddles.

**2.** Why does Ben pack extra socks?

- Ⓕ His brother borrowed his socks last time.
- ● Ⓖ He is worried that his feet will get cold at night.
- Ⓗ He wants to share the socks with his friend.
- Ⓘ His dad asks him to pack the socks.

TOTAL SCORE: _____ /4

Name _____

## Homophones

▲ Choose the best answer to each question.

**1.** Read this sentence.

> All of their shoes were untied.

What is the meaning of the word *their* in this sentence?

Ⓐ at a certain place

Ⓑ in that case

Ⓒ unlike any other

**Ⓓ** belonging to them

**2.** Read this sentence.

> Your homework is due tomorrow.

What is the meaning of the word *due* in this sentence?

Ⓕ to perform something

**Ⓖ** expected at a certain time

Ⓗ tiny drops of water

Ⓘ to be late

**3.** Read this sentence.

> Who has the right answer to this question?

What is the meaning of the word *right* in this sentence?

**Ⓐ** correct

Ⓑ a direction

Ⓒ to behave with honor

Ⓓ to make a mark on paper

---

Name _____

**3.** What happens when Ben finishes packing?

**Ⓐ** His backpack is too full.

Ⓑ He leaves for his trip.

Ⓒ He packs his raincoat.

Ⓓ He takes socks out of his bag.

**4.** What happens when Ben realizes that he forgot his flashlight?

**Ⓕ** He takes out his baseball and baseball glove.

Ⓖ He asks his dad to pack a flashlight for him.

Ⓗ He decides to leave his flashlight at home.

Ⓘ He finds a bigger bag to hold everything he needs.

TOTAL SCORE: _____ /4

## Robust Vocabulary

▲ **Choose the word that best completes each sentence.**

1. I hoped that the bike I wanted would be _____.
   - Ⓐ affordable
   - Ⓑ visible
   - Ⓒ effective
   - Ⓓ flustered

2. Cameron _____ me to come closer to tell me her secret.
   - Ⓕ contented
   - Ⓖ beckoned
   - Ⓗ mentioned
   - Ⓘ transferred

3. Each piece of candy in the box was _____ wrapped.
   - Ⓐ ridiculously
   - Ⓑ affordable
   - Ⓒ eagerly
   - Ⓓ individually

4. When the actor forgot her lines, she became _____.
   - Ⓕ affordable
   - Ⓖ flustered
   - Ⓗ visible
   - Ⓘ effective

5. Her shelves were covered with _____.
   - Ⓐ presentation
   - Ⓑ clutter
   - Ⓒ emotion
   - Ⓓ absence

Robust Vocabulary

© Harcourt • Grade 3

259

---

4. Read this sentence.

   **I could eat that whole plate of brownies.**

   What is the meaning of the word *whole* in this sentence?
   - Ⓕ complete, including all parts
   - Ⓖ a hollow space in the ground
   - Ⓗ a small bay on the coast
   - Ⓘ an opening in something

5. Read this sentence.

   **The fly buzzed against the window.**

   What is the meaning of the word *fly* in this sentence?
   - Ⓐ an opening to a tent
   - Ⓑ a small bug with wings
   - Ⓒ to move freely
   - Ⓓ to travel through the air

TOTAL SCORE: _____ /5

Homophones

© Harcourt • Grade 3

258

---

## Grammar: Past-Tense and Future-Tense Verbs

▲ Choose the best answer for each question.

1. What is the past tense of the verb *swim?*
   - Ⓐ swam
   - Ⓑ swims
   - Ⓒ will swim
   - Ⓓ swimming

2. What is the past tense of the verb *dance?*
   - Ⓕ will dance
   - Ⓖ dances
   - Ⓗ dancing
   - Ⓘ danced

3. What is the future tense of the verb *walk?*
   - Ⓐ walks
   - Ⓑ walked
   - Ⓒ will walk
   - Ⓓ walking

4. What is the future tense of the verb *hike?*
   - Ⓕ will hike
   - Ⓖ hiked
   - Ⓗ hikes
   - Ⓘ hiking

Grammar: Past-Tense and
Future-Tense Verbs
© Harcourt • Grade 3

TOTAL SCORE: _____ /4

261

---

6. The sky is dark because the moon is not _____ tonight.
   - Ⓕ visible
   - Ⓖ flustered
   - Ⓗ affordable
   - Ⓘ effective

7. What did Nicholas _____ that hurt Sandy's feelings?
   - Ⓐ remark
   - Ⓑ inherit
   - Ⓒ collaborate
   - Ⓓ beckoned

8. April's _____ was about her science fair project.
   - Ⓕ clutter
   - Ⓖ effort
   - Ⓗ detail
   - Ⓘ presentation

9. Tamara _____ that the homework was due today.
   - Ⓐ mentioned
   - Ⓑ beckoned
   - Ⓒ transferred
   - Ⓓ collaborated

10. We all agreed that her idea was an _____ solution.
    - Ⓕ affordable
    - Ⓖ inherit
    - Ⓗ effective
    - Ⓘ absence

Robust Vocabulary
© Harcourt • Grade 3

TOTAL SCORE: _____ /10

260

## Oral Reading Fluency

"Kimberly, are you ready? We don't want to be late to | 11

meet the others," Kimberly's mother called to her. | 19

Kimberly agreed that she didn't want to be late. They | 29

were going camping with three other families from their | 38

neighborhood. Kimberly had never been camping before, | 45

but she knew that she would have fun because her three | 56

best friends were going, too. | 61

Yesterday, she and her friends had spent hours | 69

planning their camping trip. Cameron was looking | 76

forward to fishing in the lake. Kimberly wanted to fish, | 86

too, but she didn't have a fishing pole. Cameron said that | 97

he had an extra pole that she could borrow. | 106

Nadia wanted to hike through the woods. She had | 115

checked out a library book to help them identify different | 125

animal tracks. Kimberly thought that sounded like fun. | 133

Kelley had been camping last year. Her family had | 142

taken a boat across the lake. Kimberly had never been on | 153

a boat before, and she was excited about her first boat | 164

trip. | 165

As Kimberly raced down the hall, her dad asked, "Are | 175

you ready?" | 177

"Ready?" she asked. "I can hardly wait!" | 184

_____ /WCPM

---

## Selection Comprehension

▲ Choose the best answer for each question.

1. At the beginning, why don't Diz and Cosmo have real dogs?
   - Ⓐ They would rather have dogs that do homework.
   - Ⓑ Robodogs are more cuddly than real dogs.
   - Ⓒ They don't like dogs that whine or bark.
   - **Ⓓ There are no real dogs on the earth.**

2. How does Cosmo first learn about real dogs?
   - Ⓕ The Professor tells Cosmo about real dogs.
   - Ⓖ Cosmo reads about real dogs in a book.
   - **Ⓗ Cosmo sees a real dog in a movie.**
   - Ⓘ Diz shows Cosmo his real dog.

3. Which idea BEST shows that the story takes place in
   the future?
   - Ⓐ Families watch movies.
   - **Ⓑ People have flying cars.**
   - Ⓒ Children eat sandwiches.
   - Ⓓ Children play with dogs.

4. What can you tell about robodogs?
   - **Ⓕ They obey only their owner.**
   - Ⓖ They do what anyone asks.
   - Ⓗ They never take a rest.
   - Ⓘ They are very loving.

5. How are robodogs and real dogs the SAME?

(A) Both can do tricks.

(B) Both can make meals.

(C) Both can speak words.

(D) Both can show feelings.

6. Who gives Diz his first real dog?

(F) Cosmo

(G) Robodog

(H) the Professor

(I) Captain Spacely

7. How do Cosmo and Diz probably feel when they get real dogs?

(A) calm

(B) disappointed

(C) frightened

(D) happy

8. What are Cosmo and Diz MOST LIKELY to do next?

(F) send their real dogs to Planet Fido

(G) teach their real dogs to clean rooms

(H) have fun playing with their real dogs

(I) start liking robodogs better than real dogs

---

READ
THINK
EXPLAIN **Written Response** (worth two points)

9. How do Diz and Cosmo's feelings about real dogs change in the story? Use information and details from "Robodogs of Greenville" to help you explain.

**Sample two-point response: They start to like real dogs**

**better because real dogs are more like friends.**

_____

_____

TOTAL SCORE: _____ /8 + _____ /2

---

Name _____

# Robust Vocabulary

▲ **Choose the word that best completes each sentence.**

**1.** My new desk will be helpful because it is _____.

   Ⓐ realistic

   🅑 functional

   Ⓒ confused

   Ⓓ flustered

**2.** My teacher _____ that we complete our homework.

   🅕 required

   Ⓖ inherited

   Ⓗ transferred

   Ⓘ responsibility

**3.** I was still _____ after the teacher explained the assignment.

   Ⓐ ample

   🅑 confused

   Ⓒ futuristic

   Ⓓ functional

**4.** The nervous boy was _____ from foot to foot.

   🅕 shifting

   Ⓖ collaborating

   Ⓗ functional

   Ⓘ dozing

**5.** Deondra felt ready for the _____ of taking care of a dog.

   Ⓐ clutter

   🅑 responsibility

   Ⓒ presentation

   Ⓓ amazement

Robust Vocabulary

© Harcourt • Grade 3

266

---

Name _____

**6.** The _____ game included spaceships and flying cars.

   🅕 ample

   🅖 futuristic

   Ⓗ effective

   Ⓘ functional

**7.** The movie about bears living in the woods was _____.

   🅐 realistic

   Ⓑ ample

   Ⓒ confused

   Ⓓ functional

**8.** Mom said there was _____ time to do our homework.

   🅕 ample

   Ⓖ functional

   Ⓗ futuristic

   Ⓘ confused

**9.** Large yellow bees are the _____ of this hive.

   Ⓐ required

   Ⓑ emotions

   Ⓒ surroundings

   🅓 inhabitants

**10.** We watched the woman on the tightrope with _____.

   🅕 responsibility

   Ⓖ clutter

   🅗 amazement

   Ⓘ presentation

Robust Vocabulary

© Harcourt • Grade 3

267

TOTAL SCORE: _____ /10

---

## Selection Comprehension

▲ **Choose the best answer for each question.**

1. How can readers tell that "Charlotte's Web" is a fantasy?
   - Ⓐ It has a plot that teaches a lesson.
   - Ⓑ The events could not happen in real life.
   - Ⓒ The story tells about real people from history.
   - Ⓓ It gives facts and information about a subject.

2. Why does Wilbur want to spin a web?
   - Ⓕ He wants to teach Charlotte to weave.
   - Ⓖ He wants to make a gift for Fern.
   - Ⓗ He knows that he is good at it.
   - Ⓘ He thinks it will be fun.

3. What can readers tell about Wilbur?
   - Ⓐ He does not give up easily.
   - Ⓑ He saves string to use for webs.
   - Ⓒ He worries about where to get food.
   - Ⓓ He has always wanted to spin a web.

4. How are Charlotte and Fern ALIKE?
   - Ⓕ Both are spiders.
   - Ⓖ Both can weave.
   - Ⓗ Both live in the barn.
   - Ⓘ Both are fond of Wilbur.

5. How does Wilbur MOST LIKELY feel after he crashes with a thud for the second time?
   - Ⓐ lucky
   - Ⓑ proud
   - Ⓒ foolish
   - Ⓓ curious

6. Charlotte can BEST be described as
   - Ⓕ selfish.
   - Ⓖ lively.
   - Ⓗ loud.
   - Ⓘ wise.

7. Which sentence BEST tells the lesson Wilbur learns in the story?
   - Ⓐ Everyone has different talents.
   - Ⓑ A true friend never leaves.
   - Ⓒ Practice brings success.
   - Ⓓ Trust is hard to earn.

8. What is MOST LIKELY to happen next?
   - Ⓕ Wilbur will try to spin a web again.
   - Ⓖ Wilbur and Charlotte will keep talking.
   - Ⓗ Wilbur will visit the Queensborough Bridge.
   - Ⓘ Wilbur will borrow more string from Templeton.

Name _____

## Phonics/Spelling: Suffixes -*tion*, -*sion*

▲ Choose the word or words that correctly complete each sentence.

1. My sister is proud of her _____ of seashells.
   - (A) collection
   - (B) recollect
   - (C) collect
   - (D) collects

2. I think I made the right _____.
   - (F) decide
   - (G) undecided
   - (H) decided
   - (I) decision

3. That is a very important _____.
   - (A) reinvent
   - (B) invention
   - (C) invent
   - (D) inventing

4. Do you know which _____ my house is in?
   - (F) directly
   - (G) direct
   - (H) direction
   - (I) redirect

Phonics/Spelling: Suffixes -*tion*, -*sion*
© Harcourt • Grade 3

271      TOTAL SCORE: _____ /4

---

Name _____

READ
THINK
EXPLAIN

## Written Response (worth two points)

9. Do you think Charlotte did the right thing when she encouraged Wilbur to spin a web? Use information and details from "Charlotte's Web" to help you explain why or why not.

**Sample two-point response: Yes, I think Charlotte did the right thing. She knew Wilbur couldn't spin a web, but he would keep thinking he could unless she made him try it. That proved it was something spiders can do but pigs can't.**

Selection Comprehension
"Charlotte's Web"
© Harcourt • Grade 3

270      TOTAL SCORE: _____ /8 + _____ /2

## Focus Skill: Make Inferences

▲ Read the passage. Then choose the best answer for each question.

As Billy walked home from school on Friday, he noticed the piles of leaves forming in his neighbors' yards. He knew that he would be raking the leaves in his own yard the next day.

On Saturday morning, Billy gathered everything he needed. He found gloves, a rake, a broom, and a box of leaf bags. When he opened the leaf bags, he saw that they were decorated with eyes, noses, and big crooked smiles. Billy worked for two hours, until the yard was perfectly cleared.

He looked at his work and saw that he had filled eight leaf bags. He carried them to the curb. He looked at the pile of stuffed bags. He laughed at how much they looked like huge pumpkins.

As Billy was picking up his tools, one of the neighbors walked over. The neighbor looked at Billy's yard, and then he said he wished Billy would rake his yard, too.

1. In which season does this story take place?

Ⓐ summer
🅑 fall
Ⓒ spring
Ⓓ winter

2. What do you already know about this season?

Ⓕ Trees have green leaves.
Ⓖ Snow covers tree branches.
🅗 Leaves fall from the trees.
Ⓘ Trees grow many new leaves.

3. What color were the leaf bags?

🅐 orange
Ⓑ brown
Ⓒ black
Ⓓ gray

4. Why did the neighbor want Billy to rake his leaves?

Ⓕ The neighbor hated raking.
🅖 The neighbor thought that Billy had done a good job.
Ⓗ The neighbor thought that Billy needed the exercise.
Ⓘ The neighbor felt sorry for Billy.

TOTAL SCORE: _____ /4

Name _____

## Multiple-Meaning Words

▲ **Read each sentence. Choose the best definition of the underlined word as used in the sentence.**

1. I swung the bat as hard as I could, but I missed the ball.
   - Ⓐ a small, flying animal
   - Ⓑ to strike something
   - Ⓒ a stick used to hit a ball
   - Ⓓ to wink or flutter

2. I have to use my ruler in math class.
   - Ⓕ someone who rules a country
   - Ⓖ a group that makes decisions and laws
   - Ⓗ a flat piece of wood, plastic, or metal used for measuring
   - Ⓘ a principle set to guide behavior and action

3. I hurt my elbow when I fell on the hard ground.
   - Ⓐ slowly and with difficulty
   - Ⓑ very firm and solid
   - Ⓒ with a great deal of force
   - Ⓓ involving a great deal of labor

4. Sara got a new dress to wear to the ball.
   - Ⓕ a round object
   - Ⓖ to make round
   - Ⓗ to throw
   - Ⓘ a large dance

Name _____

5. There was just a bit of pie left in the pan.
   - Ⓐ a small amount of something
   - Ⓑ a metal bar in a horse's mouth, attached to reins
   - Ⓒ a tiny amount of computer information
   - Ⓓ the piece on the end of a drill

6. The tiger had a thick, shiny coat.
   - Ⓕ an item of clothing
   - Ⓖ an animal's fur
   - Ⓗ a thin layer
   - Ⓘ a protective cover

7. I borrowed a pen to sign my name.
   - Ⓐ a small fenced area for animals
   - Ⓑ an instrument used for writing
   - Ⓒ to keep something in an area
   - Ⓓ to write something

8. The shy calf hid behind its mother in the field.
   - Ⓕ a young whale
   - Ⓖ part of the leg
   - Ⓗ a very young cow
   - Ⓘ a large piece of ice

TOTAL SCORE: _____ /8

# Robust Vocabulary

▲ Choose the word that best completes each sentence.

1. I told Mom that my brother was being a _____.
   - Ⓐ presentation
   - Ⓑ nuisance
   - Ⓒ require
   - Ⓓ dreadful

2. My teacher was _____ that we all follow his rules.
   - Ⓕ inevitable
   - Ⓖ sedentary
   - Ⓗ bristly
   - Ⓘ adamant

3. My dog's coat felt _____ after her haircut.
   - Ⓐ bristly
   - Ⓑ adamant
   - Ⓒ inevitable
   - Ⓓ sedentary

4. The huge sign started to _____ in the wind.
   - Ⓕ oblige
   - Ⓖ sway
   - Ⓗ require
   - Ⓘ confuse

5. My cousin is always _____ about how strong he is.
   - Ⓐ collaborating
   - Ⓑ inheriting
   - Ⓒ boasting
   - Ⓓ summoning

6. All of a sudden we heard a _____ sound.
   - Ⓕ sedentary
   - Ⓖ confuse
   - Ⓗ bristly
   - Ⓘ dreadful

7. When I am sick, I like to be _____.
   - Ⓐ sway
   - Ⓑ sedentary
   - Ⓒ inevitable
   - Ⓓ adamant

8. The sound of the bell was _____ us back to class.
   - Ⓕ boasting
   - Ⓖ mentioning
   - Ⓗ humoring
   - Ⓘ summoning

9. Will you please _____ me by agreeing to come along?
   - Ⓐ oblige
   - Ⓑ sway
   - Ⓒ confuse
   - Ⓓ require

10. The _____ day of the math test had come.
   - Ⓕ inevitable
   - Ⓖ adamant
   - Ⓗ bristly
   - Ⓘ sedentary

## Grammar: Irregular Verbs

▲ Choose the word that correctly completes each sentence.

1. Last week my mom _____ me to soccer practice.

   Ⓐ driven
   Ⓑ drove
   Ⓒ drived
   Ⓓ drive

2. I had _____ the ball into the hoop at least fifty times.

   Ⓕ threw
   Ⓖ throw
   Ⓗ thrown
   Ⓘ through

3. Because we were late, we _____ down the hall.

   Ⓐ run
   Ⓑ ran
   Ⓒ runned
   Ⓓ ranned

4. The last time I _____ peanut butter cookies to school, everyone enjoyed them.

   Ⓕ brought
   Ⓖ bring
   Ⓗ brung
   Ⓘ bringed

Grammar: Irregular Verbs

© Harcourt • Grade 3

278

TOTAL SCORE: _____ /4

## Oral Reading Fluency

| | |
|---|---|
| Cam did not enjoy her weekend chores. She wanted to | 10 |
| help around the house as her brother and sister did. Still, | 21 |
| she dreaded every Saturday morning. | 26 |
| Her mother let Cam try different chores each week, | 35 |
| hoping to find one that Cam might enjoy. First, Cam tried | 46 |
| laundry. After she turned her father's white work shirts | 55 |
| pink, her mother decided that Cam's older brother Mark | 64 |
| should probably keep doing the laundry. | 70 |
| Next, Cam tried vacuuming. She got a pair of socks | 80 |
| stuck in the vacuum cleaner by accident. Cam's sister, | 89 |
| Libby, took over after that. | 94 |
| Cam was sad. She felt that nothing she did helped her | 105 |
| family. | 106 |
| Then one Saturday morning, Cam's mother had an | 114 |
| idea. "Cam, why don't you help me weed the garden?" | 124 |
| Cam had never worked in the garden before, but she | 134 |
| liked being outside. She put on gardening gloves and | 143 |
| followed her mother outside. | 147 |
| After a few hours, Cam was still hard at work, but she | 159 |
| was enjoying herself. | 162 |
| "Cam, you did a great job!" her mother said happily. | 172 |
| "I think we have found the right chore for you." | 182 |

_____ /WCPM

Oral Reading Fluency

© Harcourt • Grade 3

279

Name _____

## Selection Comprehension

▲ Choose the best answer for each question.

1. How can readers tell that "Spiders and Their Webs" is expository nonfiction?

   (A) It has facts and information about a subject.

   (B) The events could never happen in real life.

   (C) It has animals that act like people.

   (D) The plot teaches a lesson.

2. Why did the author write "Spiders and Their Webs"?

   (F) to explain how spiders change as they grow

   (G) to teach about different kinds of spiders

   (H) to warn that spiders are dangerous

   (I) to tell a scary story about a spider

3. How are most of the spiders described in the article ALIKE?

   (A) They catch insects.

   (B) They eat fish and frogs.

   (C) They live in Costa Rica.

   (D) They are very small.

4. What is unusual about the web of the golden orb weaver?

   (F) It is stretchy.

   (G) It is underwater.

   (H) It grows on leaves.

   (I) It can be different colors.

---

Name _____

5. Which spider lives in an air-bubble house?

   (A) ray spider

   (B) water spider

   (C) golden orb weaver spider

   (D) Hawaiian happy-faced spider

6. How are the webs of the cobweb spider and the Hawaiian happy-faced spider ALIKE?

   (F) They are huge.

   (G) They are messy.

   (H) They last several days.

   (I) They are used like slingshots.

7. The author compares the web of a social spider to a garbage truck to help you understand

   (A) what size the web is.

   (B) what color the web is.

   (C) what the web feels like.

   (D) what the web is shaped like.

8. The author thinks that spiders are

   (F) funny.

   (G) harmful.

   (H) amazing.

   (I) frightening.

Name _____

## Phonics/Spelling: V/V Syllable Pattern

▲ Choose the correct way to divide each word into syllables.

1. cereal
  - Ⓐ ce-re-al
  - Ⓑ ce-real
  - Ⓒ cer-eal
  - Ⓓ c-er-eal

2. fluid
  - Ⓕ fl-uid
  - Ⓖ flui-d
  - Ⓗ flu-id
  - Ⓘ fl-ui-d

3. dial
  - Ⓐ di-a-l
  - Ⓑ dia-l
  - Ⓒ d-ial
  - Ⓓ di-al

4. lion
  - Ⓕ lio-n
  - Ⓖ l-ion
  - Ⓗ li-on
  - Ⓘ li-o-n

TOTAL SCORE: _____ /4

---

Name _____

READ THINK EXPLAIN

## Written Response (worth two points)

9. Why do spiders build webs? Use information and details from "Spiders and Their Webs" to help you explain.

Sample two-point response: Spiders use their webs

mostly to catch food to eat, like insects or even baby fish.

They also use the webs to protect their eggs. Sometimes

they use the web to wrap food up to store it until later.

TOTAL SCORE: _____ /8 + _____ /2

## Focus Skill: Make Inferences

🔺 **Read the passage. Then choose the best answer for each question.**

When Stacy woke up, it was still dark. She could have slept late, but she was too excited to go back to sleep. She thought hard as she ate breakfast. She had two entire weeks off from school. What could she do with all that time? She saw her library book on the table. She could go to the library and find more books to read. Stacy loved checking out books from the library. She'd have to wait for her mother to take her to the library, though. What else could she do?

Stacy's dog, Sniffles, put his head on Stacy's knee. She could take Sniffles for a walk. He loved going to the park. Stacy looked out the kitchen window and saw her neighbor, Mrs. Olsen, getting her newspaper. Mrs. Olsen carried a beautiful umbrella. Stacy decided that today wasn't the best day for a walk.

Stacy decided to make a list of all her favorite things to do. She knew she'd have time to do them all over the next two weeks!

1. What time of day does this story take place?
   - Ⓐ in the morning
   - Ⓑ in the afternoon
   - Ⓒ during the evening
   - Ⓓ late at night

2. Why could Stacy sleep late?
   - Ⓕ She does not have to let her dog out.
   - Ⓖ She does not have to get ready for school.
   - Ⓗ She does not feel well and needs to rest.
   - Ⓘ She does not want to eat breakfast.

3. Why might Stacy look forward to checking library books out?
   - Ⓐ Stacy is friends with the librarian.
   - Ⓑ Stacy knows how to use a computer.
   - Ⓒ Stacy wants to go to the park.
   - Ⓓ Stacy likes to read.

4. Why does Stacy decide that it is not a good day to walk Sniffles?
   - Ⓕ It is too cold.
   - Ⓖ It is raining.
   - Ⓗ It is too hot.
   - Ⓘ It is very windy.

TOTAL SCORE: _____ /4

*Student Edition* pp. 284–285

Name _____

## Multiple-Meaning Words

▲ **Read each sentence. Choose the best definition of the underlined word as used in the sentence.**

1. Lamps light the park.
   - Ⓐ to start a fire
   - Ⓑ to make bright
   - Ⓒ weighing very little
   - Ⓓ made of thin material

2. My brother forgot his watch, so he asked me what time it was.
   - Ⓕ a small clock worn on the wrist
   - Ⓖ to look at something closely
   - Ⓗ to guard something
   - Ⓘ a period of time

3. That test was a breeze after we had studied so much.
   - Ⓐ a gentle wind
   - Ⓑ to move quickly
   - Ⓒ very easy
   - Ⓓ dust from coal

4. I lost my key to the front door.
   - Ⓕ a list of symbols for a map
   - Ⓖ a piece of metal used to open a lock
   - Ⓗ a button on a computer
   - Ⓘ a list of answers

Name _____

5. The snow-covered mountains were a beautiful sight.
   - Ⓐ the power to see
   - Ⓑ something interesting to view
   - Ⓒ to measure something
   - Ⓓ to notice someone

6. His teacher told Mark's parents that Mark was a very bright student.
   - Ⓕ smart
   - Ⓖ giving off light
   - Ⓗ colorful
   - Ⓘ a clear sound

7. The pitcher threw the ball to the catcher.
   - Ⓐ a container used to pour drinks
   - Ⓑ a baseball player
   - Ⓒ a small paving stone
   - Ⓓ a part of a leaf

8. The third graders file into the room when the second bell rings.
   - Ⓕ a folder for papers
   - Ⓖ a tool for making things smooth
   - Ⓗ a piece of computer information
   - Ⓘ a line of people, one behind the other

TOTAL SCORE: _____ /8

6. The painting had an _____ design.
   - (F) elaborate
   - (G) obliges
   - (H) invent
   - (I) adamant

7. It takes hours to weave _____ of wool into a rug by hand.
   - (A) efforts
   - (B) strands
   - (C) tasks
   - (D) nuisances

8. The staircase had a _____ shape.
   - (F) sedentary
   - (G) social
   - (H) spiral
   - (I) sways

9. The judge worked to make sure there was _____.
   - (A) justice
   - (B) task
   - (C) prey
   - (D) nuisance

10. Making my bed is a _____ I do every day.
    - (F) prey
    - (G) nuisance
    - (H) justice
    - (I) task

TOTAL SCORE: _____ /10

---

# Robust Vocabulary

▲ Choose the word that best completes each sentence.

1. The fisher _____ in the catch.
   - (A) strands
   - (B) obliges
   - (C) reels
   - (D) sways

2. Jack is friendly and is comfortable in any _____ setting.
   - (F) shallow
   - (G) inventive
   - (H) social
   - (I) elaborate

3. Mrs. Jenks said that my science project was very _____.
   - (A) inventive
   - (B) shallow
   - (C) social
   - (D) elaborate

4. The _____ river was easy to wade across.
   - (F) elaborate
   - (G) shallow
   - (H) social
   - (I) inventive

5. The hungry lion hunted for _____.
   - (A) task
   - (B) justice
   - (C) nuisance
   - (D) prey

## Grammar: Adverbs

1. What is the adverb in this sentence?

   **The dancer moved gracefully.**

   Ⓐ The
   Ⓑ dancer
   Ⓒ moved
   Ⓓ gracefully

2. What is the adverb in this sentence?

   **My friends will be here in five minutes.**

   Ⓕ My
   Ⓖ will
   Ⓗ here
   Ⓘ be

3. What is the adverb in this sentence?

   **I worked hard to prepare for the test.**

   Ⓐ I
   Ⓑ worked
   Ⓒ hard
   Ⓓ to

4. What is the adverb in this sentence?

   **After the play, the crowd clapped loudly.**

   Ⓕ the
   Ⓖ play
   Ⓗ clapped
   Ⓘ loudly

**Grammar: Adverbs**

290

TOTAL SCORE: _____ /4

---

## Oral Reading Fluency

When Clarence was in first grade, he was not happy. — 10

"I am the shortest boy in my class, and it's terrible not — 22

to be tall," Clarence used to say to his parents during — 33

dinner. — 34

When Clarence was in second grade, he WAS taller, — 43

much taller. Now, though, he was upset because he could — 53

not run as fast as the other kids. — 61

"I am so slow. Everyone passes me when we run in — 72

gym class, and it's awful to be slow," he used to tell his — 85

mom and dad during dinner. — 90

In third grade, Clarence could run faster. He found out, — 100

though, that he was not a very good speller. — 109

"I have a difficult time with spelling. I never do well on — 121

spelling tests, and it's no fun being a terrible speller," he — 132

said. — 133

Now in fourth grade, Clarence is the tallest kid and the — 144

fastest runner in his class. He is also the best speller in his — 157

entire school. — 159

"How do you feel now, Clarence?" his father asked. — 168

"You mean about being tall and running and spelling? — 177

It's no big deal," replied Clarence. — 183

/WCPM

**Oral Reading Fluency**

291

---

## Selection Comprehension

▲ Choose the best answer for each question.

1. How can readers tell that "The Science Fair" is realistic fiction?

    (A) It gives facts and details about a subject.

    (B) The author writes about his or her own life.

    (C) The characters have feelings that real people have.

    (D) It tells the reader where characters stand on a stage.

2. What can readers tell about Kevin?

    (F) He has won first prize in the science fair before.

    (G) He wishes they had done a different project.

    (H) He plans ahead and is sure of his work.

    (I) He is good friends with Mr. Shanner.

3. Which action BEST shows that Beany feels worried when the science fair judges show up?

    (A) She starts to bite her nails.

    (B) She waves to her mom and dad.

    (C) She sees Kevin look toward the gym door.

    (D) She looks at a woman hurrying into the room.

4. You can tell that the judges of the science fair like projects that are

    (F) large and grand.

    (G) thorough and correct.

    (H) exciting and colorful.

    (I) flashy and entertaining.

5. Why does Beany start reciting the times tables?

    (A) She is trying to get Kevin's attention.

    (B) She wants to keep her mind off of losing.

    (C) The numbers are part of her science project.

    (D) She is studying for a test she has after the fair.

6. How do Kevin and Beany MOST LIKELY feel at the end of the story?

    (F) disappointed

    (G) confused

    (H) bored

    (I) proud

7. Which lesson can BEST be learned from this story?

    (A) Believe in yourself.

    (B) Never make fun of others.

    (C) Break big jobs into smaller parts.

    (D) Be kind to children younger than you.

8. What is MOST LIKELY to happen next?

    (F) Beany will go to Mrs. Facinelli's office to lie down.

    (G) Beany and Kevin will give their blue ribbon away.

    (H) Beany will ask her mom to buy a new tablecloth.

    (I) Beany, Kevin, and their parents will celebrate.

## Phonics/Spelling: Suffixes -able, -ible, -less, -ous

▲ Choose the word that best completes each sentence.

1. The boring movie seemed _____.

    Ⓐ endless
    Ⓑ endous
    Ⓒ endible
    Ⓓ endable

2. Dad told me a _____ story about river rafting.

    Ⓕ remarkless
    Ⓖ remarkous
    Ⓗ remarkable
    Ⓘ remarkible

3. My little sister is very _____.

    Ⓐ flexless
    Ⓑ flexable
    Ⓒ flexous
    Ⓓ flexible

4. Riding a bike without a helmet can be _____.

    Ⓕ dangerless
    Ⓖ dangerible
    Ⓗ dangerous
    Ⓘ dangerable

Phonics/Spelling: Suffixes -able, -ible,
-less, -ous
© Harcourt • Grade 3

295

TOTAL SCORE: _____ /4

---

READ
THINK
EXPLAIN

## Written Response (worth two points)

9. Explain how Beany's and Kevin's feelings about their science project are DIFFERENT. Use details and information from "The Science Fair" to support your answer.

Sample two-point response: Kevin feels good about their

science project. He plans ahead and explains things

clearly and calmly. He knows they've done a good job.

Beany is worried about the project. She thinks everyone

else's project is better and that they should have done

things differently.

Selection Comprehension
"The Science Fair"
© Harcourt • Grade 3

294

TOTAL SCORE: _____ /8 + _____ /2

# Focus Skill: Make Predictions

▲ Read the passage. Then choose the best answer for each question.

Mark and Leo got ready at Mark's house for their soccer game. After eating a good breakfast, they warmed up. Leo balanced a soccer ball on the top of his foot. Mark stretched on the floor. Finally, the clock reached 9 o'clock. Mark grinned at Leo and asked, "Are you ready?"

1. What will Mark and Leo MOST LIKELY do next?
   Ⓐ go outside to practice
   Ⓑ leave for the soccer game
   Ⓒ turn on the television
   Ⓓ finish eating breakfast

Malcolm wanted to make Mom her favorite cookies for her birthday. He asked Dad to help. They worked while Mom was gone. When Mom came home, the house smelled like cookies. "Happy birthday!" Malcolm said happily. Mom hugged him as he led her into the kitchen.

2. What will Mom MOST LIKELY do next?
   Ⓕ eat the cookies
   Ⓖ play a game
   Ⓗ go outside
   Ⓘ go to the store

Samantha looked at the sky. It was becoming dark and gray clouds were forming. The wind began to blow and the leaves on the big maple tree began to rustle. Then Samantha saw a bright flash in the distance. Without waiting for another sign, Samantha ran inside her house.

3. What will MOST LIKELY happen next?
   Ⓐ The sun will come out.
   Ⓑ Samantha will open a window.
   Ⓒ It will start to rain.
   Ⓓ Samantha will go back outside.

Tim let his dog, Max, outside. Max wouldn't go far because a fence surrounded the backyard. Tim blinked and suddenly Max had disappeared. Then Tim noticed the gate in the fence was open.

Tim went out front and called Max's name. He heard "Woof!" It was Max, playing in the neighbor's yard.

4. What will MOST LIKELY happen next?
   Ⓕ Max will be too afraid to go outside any more.
   Ⓖ Tim won't check the gate when he lets Max out.
   Ⓗ Tim's mom will only let Tim walk Max on a leash.
   Ⓘ Tim will make sure the gate is closed from now on.

TOTAL SCORE: _____ /4

# Homographs

▲ Read each sentence. They choose the best answer for each question.

1. Read this sentence.

   **I dove to catch the ball.**

   What is the meaning of the word *dove* in this sentence?

   Ⓐ a wild bird
   ⬤Ⓑ past tense of *dive*
   Ⓒ a person who hates war
   Ⓓ a gentle woman

2. Read this sentence.

   **Lydia is a very kind person.**

   What is the meaning of the word *kind* in this sentence?

   Ⓕ plenty of
   Ⓖ goods taken in place of money
   Ⓗ type of
   ⬤Ⓘ loving

3. Read this sentence.

   **I helped my dad change the tire on the car.**

   What is the meaning of the word *tire* in this sentence?

   ⬤Ⓐ rubber around a wheel
   Ⓑ became sleepy
   Ⓒ clothing
   Ⓓ wear out

4. Read this sentence.

   **I think we are close to my grandma's house.**

   What is the meaning of the word *close* in this sentence?

   Ⓕ shut
   Ⓖ same
   ⬤Ⓗ near
   Ⓘ apart

5. Read this sentence.

   **My family always goes to the state fair.**

   What is the meaning of the word *fair* in this sentence?

   Ⓐ without much wind
   Ⓑ by the rules
   Ⓒ beautiful to the eye
   ⬤Ⓓ a yearly outdoor event

TOTAL SCORE: _____ /5

## Robust Vocabulary

▲ Choose the word that best completes each sentence.

**1.** Rick needed to give his room a _____ cleaning.

Ⓐ confuse
Ⓑ social
Ⓒ thorough
Ⓓ grainy

**2.** I like my grandma because she has a great sense of _____.

Ⓕ deliberation
Ⓖ preparation
Ⓗ humor
Ⓘ gimmick

**3.** She said that I should _____ my report with more research.

Ⓐ expand
Ⓑ erupt
Ⓒ confuse
Ⓓ invent

**4.** It can be difficult to copy _____ old photos.

Ⓕ bristly
Ⓖ grainy
Ⓗ spiral
Ⓘ thorough

**5.** If you could travel _____, where would you go?

Ⓐ adamantly
Ⓑ expand
Ⓒ socially
Ⓓ abroad

**6.** After some _____, I have decided to go.

Ⓕ deliberation
Ⓖ humor
Ⓗ task
Ⓘ strand

**7.** The pressure deep inside Earth made the volcano _____.

Ⓐ reel
Ⓑ erupt
Ⓒ bristle
Ⓓ grainy

**8.** We _____ the glitter on the paper.

Ⓕ humored
Ⓖ dazed
Ⓗ sprinkled
Ⓘ boasted

**9.** The restaurant used the _____ of giving away free shirts to get new customers.

Ⓐ deliberation
Ⓑ humor
Ⓒ preparation
Ⓓ gimmick

**10.** The surprise party took plenty of _____.

Ⓕ humor
Ⓖ preparation
Ⓗ justice
Ⓘ gimmick

TOTAL SCORE: _____ /10

## Grammar: Contractions

▲ **Read each sentence. Choose the words that are
combined to make each underlined contraction.**

1. It'll be a long time before we get there.

   (A) It is

   (B) I will

   (C) It can

   (D) It will

2. They're going to arrive after seven.

   (F) They will

   (G) They sure

   (H) They are

   (I) They care

3. I didn't want to get in their way.

   (A) will not

   (B) did not

   (C) do not

   (D) does not

4. We've more to talk about.

   (F) We have

   (G) We give

   (H) We will

   (I) We are

TOTAL SCORE: _____ /4

---

## Oral Reading Fluency

| | |
|---|---|
| On a class trip to the seashore, Callie and Tina | 10 |
| searched for shells and rocks on the beach. Callie found | 20 |
| an old glass soda bottle in the sand. | 28 |
| "Look at this," Callie said as she picked up the bottle. | 39 |
| "There's something in it." | 43 |
| "Probably a worm," Tina said. | 48 |
| "No, it's a note," Callie replied, digging the muddy | 57 |
| paper out of the bottle. | 62 |
| "It says it's a map to an unbelievable treasure," Callie | 72 |
| explained. "'Go to the center of City Park and face away | 83 |
| from the sun. Take 200 long steps straight ahead and | 93 |
| then turn left and take 35 short steps. Climb the stairs. | 104 |
| Straight ahead, you will find great treasure.'" | 111 |
| The next Saturday, Callie and Tina asked Callie's | 119 |
| mother to take them to City Park. They excitedly followed | 129 |
| the directions in the note. After climbing the stairs, they | 139 |
| stopped suddenly, quite surprised. Before them was a | 147 |
| beautiful building. | 149 |
| "It's City Library," Callie's mother said. | 155 |
| "I've never been here," said Tina. | 161 |
| "The treasure must be in the things you can learn from | 172 |
| books," said Callie as she and Tina raced up the library's | 183 |
| steps. | 184 |

_____ /WCPM

## Selection Comprehension

▲ Choose the best answer for each question.

1. What is "The Planets" MOST LIKE?

  Ⓐ a mystery

  Ⓑ a tall tale

  Ⓒ realistic fiction

  Ⓓ expository nonfiction

2. What is the MAIN reason the author wrote "The Planets"?

  Ⓕ to compare two planets that are alike

  Ⓖ to teach facts and details about planets

  Ⓗ to explain how planets got their names

  Ⓘ to tell a story about traveling to a planet

3. When compared with most stars, planets are

  Ⓐ brighter.

  Ⓑ smaller.

  Ⓒ hotter.

  Ⓓ older.

4. How are the planets ALIKE?

  Ⓕ They circle the sun.

  Ⓖ They are made of gas.

  Ⓗ They have days of the same length.

  Ⓘ They have nights of the same length.

5. People need a telescope to see Pluto because it is so

  Ⓐ hot.

  Ⓑ large.

  Ⓒ far away.

  Ⓓ bright.

6. What causes the tides to rise and fall?

  Ⓕ the sun

  Ⓖ the stars

  Ⓗ the moon

  Ⓘ the planets

7. What determines how long a planet's year is?

  Ⓐ how long it takes to go around the sun

  Ⓑ how close it is to the sun

  Ⓒ how many rings it has

  Ⓓ how bright it is

8. With which idea would the author MOST LIKELY agree?

  Ⓕ Earth is the only important planet.

  Ⓖ It is too dangerous to explore planets.

  Ⓗ People could live on most other planets.

  Ⓘ We need to continue studying the planets.

## Phonics/Spelling: Prefixes *bi-*, *non-*, *over-*

▲ Choose the word that correctly completes each sentence.

1. Turn off the water before the bucket _____.

Ⓐ overfills
Ⓑ refills
Ⓒ filling
Ⓓ filled

2. Karen was hoping to get a _____ flight from New York.

Ⓕ stop
Ⓖ stoppable
Ⓗ nonstop
Ⓘ stopping

3. I need new tires for my _____.

Ⓐ recycle
Ⓑ cycling
Ⓒ cycled
Ⓓ bicycle

4. They gave me a little money back after I was _____ for the book.

Ⓕ recharged
Ⓖ discharged
Ⓗ overcharged
Ⓘ charging

TOTAL SCORE: _____ /4

---

READ
THINK
EXPLAIN

## Written Response (worth two points)

9. **COMPARING TEXTS** Suppose Jeremy in "Jeremy's House" really lived in a house with no roof. What could he see in the night sky? Use details from BOTH "The Planets" and "Jeremy's House" to describe what he could see.

Sample two-point response: Jeremy could see stars and

planets in the sky. The stars would twinkle. If he saw

Mars, it might look red. If he used a telescope, he might

see the planets that are far away. He could see our moon.

If he tried to count the stars, it would take him forever

because there are so many.

TOTAL SCORE: _____ /8 + _____ /8

---

# Focus Skill: Make Predictions

🔺 **Read the passage. Then choose the best answer for each question.**

Danielle was sad. She was supposed to go to the beach today, but it was raining.

Dad walked into the room and said, "We can still have fun."

Your favorite author is speaking at the library today."

Danielle smiled. "I'll get the umbrellas," she said.

**1.** What will Danielle and Dad MOST LIKELY do next?

Ⓐ go to the beach

Ⓑ go to the library

Ⓒ go shopping

Ⓓ stay at home

Charles had lost his watch. He searched the entire house but had no luck. He explained his problem to his brother, Nick.

"Maybe you left it at Grandma's house," Nick offered.

"There's only one way to find out," Charles said, racing for the phone.

**2.** What will Charles MOST LIKELY do next?

Ⓕ search his house again

Ⓖ thank his brother for his help

Ⓗ find his watch under the sofa

Ⓘ call his grandmother about his watch

---

Emily wants to be on the school running team. She practices almost every day. Soon she is running faster than her brother, Aaron. Aaron is already on the team.

Finally the running team tryouts come. Emily does her best and wins every race. Then she sees the smiling coach walking toward her.

**3.** What will MOST LIKELY happen next?

Ⓐ The coach will challenge Emily to another race.

Ⓑ Emily will decide she doesn't want to join the team.

Ⓒ Aaron and Emily will race to see who makes the team.

Ⓓ The coach will ask Emily to join the running team.

Zach was getting off the bus when he found a red book on the ground. On the cover was the name "Anna B." Zach brought the book to the office and told them where he found it.

Later, when Zach was eating lunch, a girl came up to him. "Hi, I'm Anna. Did you find my book?" she asked.

**4.** What will MOST LIKELY happen next?

Ⓕ Anna will thank Zach for finding her book.

Ⓖ Zach will look for more books on the ground.

Ⓗ Anna will ask Zach to find her lost backpack.

Ⓘ Zach will put up a "found" sign for the book.

TOTAL SCORE: _____ /4

Name _____

# Homographs

▲ Choose the best answer for each question.

1. Read this sentence.

   **The pitcher is filled with water.**

   What is the meaning of the word *pitcher* in this sentence?

   Ⓐ a container used to pour liquid

   Ⓑ a baseball player

   Ⓒ a perfect example

   Ⓓ a photograph

2. Read this sentence.

   **I lead my little sister by the hand when we go for walks.**

   What is the meaning of the word *lead* in this sentence?

   Ⓕ to be at the beginning

   Ⓖ an example

   Ⓗ to show the way

   Ⓘ a type of metal

3. Read this sentence.

   **The sow in the pen had several babies.**

   What is the meaning of the word *sow* in this sentence?

   Ⓐ to plant seeds

   Ⓑ to spread something

   Ⓒ a female pig

   Ⓓ a piece of metal

---

Name _____

4. Read this sentence.

   **Meg's new dress had a tear on the sleeve.**

   What is the meaning of the word *tear* in this sentence?

   Ⓕ drop of liquid from the eye

   Ⓖ move quickly

   Ⓗ to pull apart

   Ⓘ a hole in the material

5. Read this sentence.

   **My sister tied a bow in my hair ribbon.**

   What is the meaning of the word *bow* in this sentence?

   Ⓐ a knot with loops

   Ⓑ the front of a ship

   Ⓒ a flat piece of wood with strings for playing an instrument

   Ⓓ to bend forward

TOTAL SCORE: _____ /5

Name _____

## Robust Vocabulary

▲ **Choose the word that best completes each sentence.**

1. That raccoon _____ every time we put the trash out.
   - Ⓐ reflects
   - Ⓑ erupts
   - Ⓒ appears
   - Ⓓ rotates

2. The toddler seemed to have an _____ amount of energy.
   - Ⓕ evidence
   - Ⓖ appears
   - Ⓗ infinite
   - Ⓘ abroad

3. In the middle of the dance, the dancer _____ on one foot.
   - Ⓐ rotates
   - Ⓑ appears
   - Ⓒ reels
   - Ⓓ expands

4. My line was crooked because my hand was not _____.
   - Ⓕ distinct
   - Ⓖ steady
   - Ⓗ infinite
   - Ⓘ expansive

5. The turtle rose to the _____ of the water.
   - Ⓐ gimmick
   - Ⓑ humor
   - Ⓒ evidence
   - Ⓓ surface

---

Name _____

6. The mirror _____ my image.
   - Ⓕ reflects
   - Ⓖ sprinkled
   - Ⓗ thorough
   - Ⓘ through

7. The cookie crumbs were _____ that someone had been in the kitchen.
   - Ⓐ preparation
   - Ⓑ evidence
   - Ⓒ surface
   - Ⓓ humor

8. I sorted the clothes into two _____ piles.
   - Ⓕ grainy
   - Ⓖ steady
   - Ⓗ distinct
   - Ⓘ social

9. I moved the picture _____ so that it would be straight.
   - Ⓐ slightly
   - Ⓑ appears
   - Ⓒ elaborately
   - Ⓓ social

10. The mountains are so large that they seem _____.
    - Ⓕ steady
    - Ⓖ distinct
    - Ⓗ expansive
    - Ⓘ grainy

TOTAL SCORE: _____ /10

## Grammar: Punctuation Roundup

▲ Choose the best answer for each question.

**1.** Which sentence is capitalized correctly?

Ⓐ The state of Alaska is the largest state in the United States.

Ⓑ the state of Alaska is the largest State in the United States.

Ⓒ The State of alaska is the largest state in The United States.

Ⓓ The state of Alaska is the largest state in the united states.

**2.** Which sentence is punctuated correctly?

Ⓕ My best friend likes bananas, apples and grapes.

Ⓖ My best friend likes bananas apples and grapes.

Ⓗ My best friend likes bananas, apples, and grapes.

Ⓘ My best, friend likes bananas, apples, and grapes.

**3.** Which sentence is punctuated correctly?

Ⓐ My favorite book is <u>Charlotte's Web</u>.

Ⓑ My favorite book is Charlotte's Web.

Ⓒ My favorite book is "Charlotte's Web".

Ⓓ My favorite book is Charlotte's Web.

**4.** Which sentence is punctuated correctly?

Ⓕ We sang America the Beautiful at the assembly.

Ⓖ We sang "America the Beautiful" at the assembly.

Ⓗ We sang America the Beautiful at the assembly.

Ⓘ We sang America the Beautiful at the assembly.

Grammar: Punctuation Roundup     314     TOTAL SCORE: _____ /4

© Harcourt • Grade 3

---

## Oral Reading Fluency

What comes to mind when you think of a desert?    10

Do you see great hills of blowing sand? Do you imagine    21

camels with tall humps plodding slowly under a hot sun?    31

It's true that many deserts are sandy and hot. Deserts can    42

also be rocky, mountainous, or covered in snow and ice.    52

A desert is an area that gets ten or fewer inches of    64

rain each year. Deserts cover about one-fifth of Earth's    73

surface. In most deserts, temperatures during the day    81

are extremely hot. At night, the desert air becomes very    91

cool. The exceptions are the deserts of Antarctica. These    100

deserts are cold all the time.    106

The largest of all deserts is the Sahara in northern    116

Africa. The Sahara has mountains and sand dunes, but it    126

is mostly bare rock and gravel. Very few plants can grow    137

in the Sahara. In certain areas, people bring water from    147

faraway rivers. This helps them grow fruits, vegetables,    155

and grains. People raising herds of sheep and goats in the    166

desert often travel between their farms and the rivers.    175

Oral Reading Fluency     315     _____ /WCPM

© Harcourt • Grade 3

Name _____

# Selection Comprehension

▲ **Choose the best answer for each question.**

1. It is dangerous to fly close to Saturn because a spaceship is likely to
   (A) get caught in a ring.
   (B) melt from the heat.
   (C) run out of power.
   (D) turn into a gas.

2. Why does the crew keep a space log?
   (F) to help remember names of the planets they visit
   (G) to describe how the crew feels about each other
   (H) to plan what to do when they reach Earth
   (I) to tell what they see on their travels

3. Why doesn't *Explorer* land on the Sun?
   (A) There isn't enough time.
   (B) The spaceship would burn up.
   (C) The crew has landed there before.
   (D) The crew would rather land on Mercury.

4. Jupiter's moon, Io, has many volcanoes because it is
   (F) rocky.
   (G) windy.
   (H) wobbly.
   (I) young.

Selection Comprehension
"Voyage Across the Solar System"
© Harcourt • Grade 3

---

Name _____

5. It is difficult to study Pluto from Earth because Pluto is
   (A) small and distant.
   (B) fast and crowded.
   (C) grainy and fuzzy.
   (D) dark and cold.

6. Why is the crew excited to get close to Pluto?
   (F) It is most like Earth.
   (G) It has beautiful ice rings.
   (H) People have not been there before.
   (I) They hope to study volcanoes there.

7. How are Earth and Mars the SAME?
   (A) Both have rings.
   (B) Both have ice caps.
   (C) Both are covered with rivers.
   (D) Both are called the Red Planet.

8. What happens when *Explorer* moves AWAY from the Sun?
   (F) It slows down.
   (G) It is in more danger.
   (H) It gets hotter inside.
   (I) It becomes hard to steer.

Selection Comprehension
"Voyage Across the Solar System"
© Harcourt • Grade 3

---

---

*Student Edition* pp. 316–317

© Harcourt • Grade 3

Name _____

## Robust Vocabulary

▲ Choose the word that best completes each sentence.

1. We found an _____ stream on one side of the river.
   - Ⓐ occur
   - Ⓑ infinite
   - Ⓒ uncharted
   - Ⓓ aligned

2. April telephoned the dentist to _____ her appointment.
   - Ⓕ preview
   - Ⓖ reflect
   - Ⓗ confirm
   - Ⓘ magnify

3. The wheels of my car were perfectly _____.
   - Ⓐ aligned
   - Ⓑ shifted
   - Ⓒ observed
   - Ⓓ sprinkled

4. If we _____ the photograph, the details will be clearer.
   - Ⓕ sway
   - Ⓖ magnify
   - Ⓗ mention
   - Ⓘ safeguard

5. My art class _____ great ideas for projects.
   - Ⓐ occur
   - Ⓑ cautions
   - Ⓒ summons
   - Ⓓ generates

Robust Vocabulary

© Harcourt • Grade 3

319

---

Name _____

READ
THINK
EXPLAIN

## Written Response (worth two points)

9. Explain why you would or would not like to be a crew member on *Explorer*. Use information and details from "Voyage Across the Solar System" to help you explain.

Sample two-point response: I wouldn't want to travel

that far from home, and I would be afraid to go near a

hot planet.

_____

_____

Selection Comprehension
"Voyage Across the Solar System"

© Harcourt • Grade 3

318

TOTAL SCORE: _____ /8 + _____ /2

---

© Harcourt • Grade 3

6. We _____ the launch of the rocket on television this morning.
   - (F) observed
   - (G) expanded
   - (H) confused
   - (I) aligned

7. Washing your hands may help _____ you from germs.
   - (A) erupt
   - (B) safeguard
   - (C) confirm
   - (D) magnify

8. Our cottage is on a _____ beach.
   - (F) disguised
   - (G) magnify
   - (H) picturesque
   - (I) reflect

9. Adam did not expect that result to _____.
   - (A) generate
   - (B) exclaim
   - (C) reflect
   - (D) occur

10. Bonnie is going on a month-long _____ to the North Pole.
    - (F) expedition
    - (G) prey
    - (H) picturesque
    - (I) evidence

**Robust Vocabulary**

320

TOTAL SCORE: _____ /10